THE GREATEST STORIES OF THE OLD WEST EVER TOLD

TRUE TALES AND LEGENDS OF FAMOUS GUNFIGHTERS, OUTLAWS AND SHERIFFS FROM THE WILD WEST

JONATHAN HUNT

ISBN: 979-8-89095-010-9

TABLE OF CONTENTS

ATTENTION:

DO YOU WANT MY FUTURE BOOKS AT
HEAVY DISCOUNTS AND EVEN FOR FREE?

HEAD OVER TO WWW.SECRETREADS.COM
AND JOIN MY SECRET BOOK CLUB!

INTRODUCTION

When most people think about the Old West, they think of what they have read or seen in Western books and movies: cowboys leading massive cattle drives across the sprawling American frontier, battles between cowboys and Indians, card playing and whiskey drinking in the saloons, and showdowns between lawmen and outlaws.

There's a reason why the Old West has become so romanticized and enduring in American literature and media today. It was a time of lawlessness and anarchy when people often had to take matters into their own hands. After all, this era was also called the "Wild West" for a reason.

But it was also a time of opportunity and self-sufficiency where people had to fend for themselves and forge their own paths to create their destinies. Hundreds of thousands of people took a great risk to migrate from the more civilized East to the wild American frontier in search of a better life. While many were able to do so for themselves and their families, many others paid the ultimate price with their lives.

This book, *The Greatest Stories of the Old West Ever Told*, covers incredible true stories about famous lawmen, outlaws, cowboys, and Native Americans who lived in this world. We will cover famous stories about the legendary gunfighter Wild Bill Hickok and how he met his untimely demise at Deadwood, the Lincoln County War that erupted into one the biggest range wars in American history, the famous gunfight at the O.K. Corral between the Earp Brothers and the Cowboy gang, and how the infamous outlaw Jesse James met his end at the hands of one of his own men.

We'll also follow lesser-known stories including the quest of the Apache warrior Geronimo for revenge against the soldiers who murdered his family, camels that were imported from Arabia into the Southwest for work, and even strange UFO sightings from cowboys and Native Americans that eerily match descriptions of UFO sightings in the present day.

The Old West was an unforgiving place and a vastly different world from the one we live in today, and yet it played such a massive role in the formation of the United

States as we know it. That's because there would be no America today if it weren't for the Old West and the men and women who lived and fought in it. These are their stories.

CUSTER'S LAST STAND

In 1876, George Armstrong Custer and his army of around 250 men found themselves surrounded and wiped out by an alliance of Native American tribes. The massacre sent shockwaves throughout America, but what tactical errors did Custer make that led to the disastrous battle?

Our first true story of the Old West takes us to the Great Plains of Montana in 1876.

Much of what would become the western part of the United States had been explored and California had already become a state in 1850, but most of the so-called "Wild West" was still untamed and wide open for the taking. Settlers and frontiersmen and women alike were moving their families westward in search of a better life, and the United States Army was leading the way.

Many towns were being established around American army outposts and, following the conclusion of the American Civil

War, the drive of the military, settlers, and colonists towards the west was accelerating at a rapid pace. People in the eastern states were entranced by the notion of forging a new life for themselves in the beautiful yet rugged lands that lay hundreds of miles to the west. To these people, the West represented anything from land to freedom to riches to the thrill of adventure.

The only real obstacle to the settlers and American military units pushing their way westward were the various hostile Native American tribes who lived throughout the frontier. The American colonists and military had already conflicted with several of these tribes for quite some time, and previous attempts at bringing about peace were met with failure.

For example, in 1830, the Indian Removal Act was initiated whereby the American government was authorized to forcefully move Indian tribes from their lands east of the Mississippi River toward the west. But only a few years later, with more settlers and frontiersmen moving westward into the Great Plains and the Rocky Mountains, they came into conflict with the same Native American tribes all over again.

The rather loose but nonetheless interconnected series of conflicts with the American military and arriving settlers on one side and the Native Indian tribes on the other became known as the American Indian Wars. While we should already all know what the outcome of these wars was, the Native tribes still managed to score several impressive victories along the way.

The Battle of the Little Bighorn fought in June 1876, was among the most colossal defeats for the United States Army in the American Indian Wars. It became infamously known as "Custer's Last Stand," named after the colonel who commanded the American forces in the engagement.

Why were the American forces so seriously defeated at Little Bighorn? What were the ramifications of the battle and what led up to it in the first place? And who was Colonel Custer?

Let's dive right in.

****

George Armstrong Custer may have graduated bottom of his class of 34 students from West Point in 1861, but that did nothing to hinder the advancement of his career in the United States Army. When the American Civil War broke out, the Union was in desperate need of trained officers as many had sided with the Confederacy.

Despite his rather poor performance at West Point, Custer was recognized by his superiors for his talents as a cavalry officer. Custer subsequently found himself promoted to Brigadier General of volunteer Union cavalry forces at the very young age of 23, and he served as a cavalry commander throughout the Civil War.

Most notably, Custer served at the famous Battle of Gettysburg and in the Overland and Shenandoah Valley campaigns. He was also present when Confederate commander Robert E. Lee surrendered to General Ulysses S. Grant at Appomattox in 1865.

In fact, Custer was somewhat responsible for the surrender of General Lee that day. When the Union army conquered the Confederate capital of Richmond in Virginia, General Lee took what remained of his army and attempted to retreat further south to continue the fight. General Custer's cavalry unit, however, blocked Lee's only plausible escape route.

Lee then provided the Confederates' first flag of truce to Custer before meeting with Grant at Appomattox to formally surrender. Had Custer failed to block Lee from escaping, the Civil War would likely have continued with even further loss of life.

Custer perhaps should have been most famous for blocking General Lee's escape route at Appomattox to bring the Civil War to a faster conclusion. But, as fate would have it, history had something else in store for Custer instead.

****

Custer took a leave of absence after his service in the Civil War, for which he was widely commended. Custer believed that he could use the clout he had gained in the war to help him forge a new career path. The only question was what that career path would be.

He traveled to New York City with his wife, Elizabeth, where he explored potential careers in the mining and railroad industries. Both of these industries were booming, and it initially seemed reasonable to Custer that he could enjoy a very lucrative career in either.

Ultimately, he realized that the life of a mining or railroad executive would not be for him. Custer then traveled to Michigan, where he considered using his reputation as a successful military officer to run for the House of Representatives. It was here that Custer attempted to display his political talents by engaging in public political debates about how the victorious Northern states should treat the Southern states; Custer argued for a policy of moderation in support of then-President Andrew Johnson with whom he would tour the South.

But fate would not allow Custer to become a politician either. Unable to gain adequate political support to mount a serious campaign (as the sentiment in the North was strongly against the South instead of the more lenient approach that Custer favored), he returned to the army and ended up becoming commissioned as a Lieutenant Colonel in the Regular Army (unlike the Volunteer forces he commanded during the Civil War). He was then dispatched westward to the Dakotas to take part in the conflicts against the Indians and was provided command of the 7th Cavalry Regiment.

In 1873, Custer began leading cavalry expeditions into the Black Hills region of South Dakota. Gold was discovered there, and when Custer made a public announcement the following year, it set off the Black Hills Gold Rush that saw thousands of people abandon their lives back east for the chance to make it rich in the Black Hills. Many of these settlers would arrive in a Black Hills frontier town called

Deadwood, which we'll discuss in later chapters of this book.

As more and more settlers came to the Dakotas seeking riches, tensions between the Americans and the Native Indian tribes became heightened even further. The Americans were pushing relentlessly west in search of land and riches, while the tribes wanted to defend their homelands. It didn't take long for tensions to escalate into violence.

Custer's 7th Cavalry Regiment engaged in multiple skirmishes with the various Native tribes living in the area, the four most prominent of which were the Arapaho, Cheyenne, Lakota, and Sioux.

This continued for about two years, until January 1876, when the United States government enacted a plan to settle the violence with the Indian tribes in the region once and for all. Ulysses Grant was now President, and his administration resolved that the United States should take official possession of the Black Hills and stop all Indian attacks.

To accomplish this, the decision was made to gather all of the free Plains Indians together into reservations. Any tribes that failed to report to their designated reservation by

January 31, 1876, would be considered hostile and an enemy of the United States.

Some tribes complied with the directions the U.S. government delivered, but others resolved to stand and fight. The American military forces in the area were ordered to regard any resisting Native American person as a hostile threat.

The stage for the Battle of Little Bighorn, where Custer would famously (or infamously) make his last stand, was now set.

****

Several bands of Arapaho, Cheyenne, Lakota, and Sioux Indians, who previously had conflicted with one another, joined forces to combat their common enemy.

Chief Sitting Bull, a Hunkpapa Lakota chief who was known for his oratorical talents, bravery, and skill in battle, called for a forceful resistance against American westward expansion and rallied these tribes together. His reputation as a daring warrior combined with his charisma made him a natural leader for the Indians who refused to go to their designated reservations.

By combining their forces, the Indian tribes put together a viable fighting force consisting of several thousand experienced warriors. Throughout the spring of 1876, more and more Indians living in the Dakotas and Montana decided to join Sitting Bull.

By June, Sitting Bull had assembled an army of between 1 and 2,500 Indian warriors from various tribes, with more reinforcements coming in by the day. He camped his army by the Little Bighorn River in the southern Montana Territory. At that year's Sun Dance (an annual healing ceremony practiced by some Native Americans in the United States and Indigenous people in Canada, mainly those of Plains cultures), Sitting Bull claimed he had a prophetic vision. He foresaw a massive victory of his people over the American army sent to hunt him down.

The United States military had received word that Sitting Bull was amassing warriors to fight against them. In response, Lieutenant General Philip Sheridan dispatched three separate army columns into the Dakotas and Montana. Their orders were simple: either take the resisting Indians to their reservations or use force and engage them in battle if they refused.

Custer's 7th Cavalry Regiment served as part of one of these military columns sent west. The commander of this particular column was Brigadier General Alfred H. Terry. Terry was acutely aware of Custer's experience and performance in the Civil War, and he believed Custer was the right man to lead a force that could track down Sitting Bull.

On June 25, 1876, Terry dispatched Custer and the 7th Cavalry into the Little Bighorn Valley in Montana. Terry's strategy was for the 7th Cavalry to engage with Sitting Bull's warriors from the south. The goal was to force Sitting Bull to retreat northward, where they would be met by another force that was positioned upstream of the Little Bighorn River.

Custer's scouts discovered Sitting Bull's village, and when they reported its location to Custer, he resolved to assault the village in a surprise attack at dawn the next day. Custer divided his regiment, which consisted of around 700 men, into three battalions each. The idea was to use all three battalions as prongs to attack Sitting Bull's forces from multiple sides at once, but the strategy would ultimately prove to be Custer's undoing.

****

Custer's plan was doomed from the start. His strategy relied on the element of surprise, but this was ruined when Sitting Bull's scouts caught sight of his forces.

Custer now had a choice to make. He could either attack immediately so Sitting Bull would not have enough time to prepare a proper defense, or he could fall back and reorganize the 7th Cavalry to come up with a revised strategy.

Apparently eager for glory, Custer elected to pursue the former option. At around noon on June 25, Custer's three battalions attacked Sitting Bull's camp and a massive battle ensued.

Based on the reports of his scouts, Custer was convinced that Sitting Bull commanded less than 800 warriors and that the two factions were fairly evenly matched in terms of numbers. In reality, Sitting Bull commanded between 1,000 to 2,500 warriors and Custer realized too late that he was gravely outnumbered.

Furthermore, Custer was also convinced that Sitting Bull's warriors were equipped primarily with primitive spears and bows and arrows. They were actually armed with the same repeating rifles and revolvers with which Custer's men were equipped.

To make matters worse, when Custer's three battalions (consisting of 200–300 men each) launched their attack, they became completely cut off from one another in the chaos and were unable to provide each other with the proper support.

In short, Custer was directly attacking a force that was many times the size of his own, had failed to anticipate how well-armed this larger force was, and had greatly weakened his own regiment by dividing them in such a way that they could not support one another.

Recognizing his folly too late, Custer was forced to go on the defensive. He called for his three battalions to go into a full fighting retreat, with all three still cut off from one another. Thousands of Sitting Bull's warriors spread out and stampeded across the plains in pursuit.

There's an old saying that to win a battle you have to divide and conquer. Custer had already committed the dividing part; now it was Sitting Bull's turn to conquer.

The battalion Custer was with, approximately 250 men strong, attempted to reach the higher ground on a hill (later known as "Custer's Hill"), but they were unable to find any respite from the continued Indian assault. Cavalrymen were dropping left and right from the Indians' rifle fire.

Eventually, Custer and his surviving men found themselves on the top of the hill and surrounded by thousands of Sitting Bull's warriors with no chance of escape.

The Indians closed in from all sides and the outcome of the battle was decided.

****

Not a single man in the battalion who retreated to Custer's Hill survived. One by one, they were all picked off until none were left. Nearly 300 U.S. cavalrymen were killed during the entire engagement.

When Custer's body was found by a U.S. army detachment days later, it was discovered he had sustained two bullet wounds: one to his temple and another right below his heart, in addition to many other blows across his body. Even though Custer had several strategic blunders that led to the total defeat of his forces, there's no question that he went down fighting with his men.

While the Battle of Little Bighorn was a significant victory for Sitting Bull, it was also short-lived. Even though the alliance of Indian tribes triumphed at Little Bighorn, their own losses were not insignificant as a few hundred warriors were either killed or wounded in the process of annihilating Custer's men. These losses were simply not replaceable for Sitting Bull, whereas the loss of Custer's battalion was replaced within weeks.

The defeat at Little Bighorn also did nothing to deter the U.S. Army. Instead, they deployed thousands of more troops and Sitting Bull's alliance was defeated within a year after subsequent battles. Sitting Bull himself evaded U.S. forces until 1881 when he was forced to surrender.

Sitting Bull would go on to work as a performer at Buffalo Bill's Wild West Show. He then returned to his original home in South Dakota. When it became feared that Sitting Bull would support the Ghost Dance movement (a spiritual Native American movement that was viewed by the American government as a threat), the local Indian Service agent ordered Sitting Bull's arrest on December 15, 1890.

A fight broke out when the arrest was attempted and Sitting Bull was shot twice in the scuffle, once in the side of the torso and again in his head. He died later that day, but

since remained an icon of Native American
against the American push west.

As for Custer, he too has remained an icon of the American West, but for different reasons than Sitting Bull. Whereas Sitting Bull is almost universally recognized for his valiant and yet doomed defiance against American expansion, views of Custer remain decidedly mixed.

Some perceive Custer as a hero who made a brave stand against overwhelming Indian forces, while others see him as an arrogant military commander who committed several obvious strategic blunders that led to his defeat.

Either way, the last stand of Custer and his men against Sitting Bull went down as one of the most legendary (and notorious) battles of the American West.

WILD BILL HICKOK

In 1876, "Wild Bill" Hickok, one of the most famous gunfighters of the Old West known for surviving gunfight after gunfight, tragically lost his life in the fabled town of Deadwood. This chapter covers Wild Bill's life leading up to his tragic demise and the reasons why he met his end.

Deadwood, South Dakota.

If there ever was a town in the old American frontier that was known for extreme lawlessness and debauchery, Deadwood was it. This was the town that was the very definition of the term "Wild West."

The settlement that eventually became known as Deadwood was established in the early 1870s.

As we discussed in the previous chapter, when Colonel Custer and his 7th Cavalry regiment were pushing west through the Black Hills in the Dakota territories in 1874, they discovered gold in the region. This set off a gold rush with thousands of settlers abandoning their lives east to travel to the Dakotas for a chance to strike it rich.

Deadwood was established around this time. Initially only a collection of tents in the mountains of the Black Hills near where gold had been found, the settlement quickly grew into a town complete with hotels, saloons, brothels, general stores, and homes. At its peak, more than 25,000 people were living there.

The town of Deadwood was controversial from the start because it was built on land that was promised to the Lakota people following the Treaty of Fort Laramie in 1868. This treaty had promised that the entire Black Hills region would be left to the Lakota people, who believed the land to be sacred. That all changed thanks to Custer when he made the public announcement that gold had been discovered in the mountains.

Controversy would continue to brew in Deadwood throughout its history. Settlers came to become miners and hopefully strike it rich, and entrepreneurs came to sell goods to the settlers.

The town quickly became known as a hub of anarchy and lawlessness. Murder, opium usage, drunkenness, and sex work were rampant throughout the town, and the hastily improvised courtrooms for trials were not known for being fair and impartial.

Deadwood is also the setting of the eponymous TV series that ran from 2004 to 2006, which helped spread knowledge about what happened in this wild and unstable town to the American public.

Many of the most famous figures of the Old West would come to Deadwood at some point in their lives. These included big names such as Calamity Jane, Seth Bullock, Al Swearengen, Wyatt Earp, and the infamous gunfighter and gambler Wild Bill Hickok, whose luck finally ran out there in 1876.

Who was Wild Bill?

****

The man we now call "Wild Bill" Hickok was first known as James Butler Hickok. Hickok was just as much a legend in his lifetime as he is now. Even though he was known for being a gunfighter and gambler, in reality, Hickok worked as a stagecoach driver, soldier, scout, wagon master, and lawman.

It was through his adventures in these career paths that he gained fame as the gunfighter and gambler that most people know him as today, and it's also where he got his famous name from. The very name "Wild Bill" is familiar even to those who are not familiar with Western history.

Hickok himself was easily recognizable for his long hair, distinctive mustache, and pair of ivory-gripped Colt 1851 Navy .36 caliber revolvers that he carried with the butts forward in a red sash around his waist. Hickok was known for his extreme speed and accuracy with these pistols, winning many duels that each added to this notoriety.

James Butler Hickok was born in Illinois in 1837 into a very religious family. His parents were very strict with him and his six siblings growing up, requiring their children to complete all their chores daily and to attend church each Sunday. It's perhaps ironic that the man who became known as "Wild Bill" grew up in a tightly disciplined household.

Before the Civil War broke out, Hickok's parents (who were passionate abolitionists) helped work on the Underground Railroad to smuggle slaves out of the South. When Hickok was a teenager, he was assisting his father smuggle out slaves in a hay wagon when they were chased by law enforcement who fired pistols at them.

Hickok was thrilled by the experience and the incident served as the start of an intense interest in guns. Hickok began practicing target shooting with his father's guns and gained a reputation as an excellent marksman in his community.

When he was 17 years old, Hickok left home to begin his career. After a stint as a towpath driver in Illinois, Hickok traveled to Kansas where he worked as a stagecoach driver transporting people on the Oregon and Santa Fe trails. During his time in Kansas, Hickok met William "Buffalo Bill" Cody, who later became famous for establishing the Buffalo Bill Wild West Show.

Working as a stagecoach driver in the 1850s was a dangerous endeavor because of the constant threat of hostile Indian tribes and outlaws who inhabited the frontier. Hickok always carried multiple firearms with him and sometimes would have to open fire against attacking Indians or bandits to protect the passengers. The marksmanship skills that he had developed in his earlier years paid off.

In one incident, Hickok and his passengers were sleeping at night when they awoke to a black bear that was attacking the stagecoach. Hickok killed the bear with a knife but not before suffering grievous injuries from the bear's claws and fangs that nearly killed him.

Even though Hickok was not expected to survive his wounds, he pulled through and returned to Kansas in the late 1850s. Hickok's fame began to build as he was known as the man who killed a bear with little more than his bare hands and who could protect stagecoaches from robbers and Indians. This became a constant theme throughout Hickok's life, as he regularly found himself in violent and intense situations that he should not have survived.

In Kansas, Hickok went to work with the Pony Express and went to work for a man named David McCanles. Hickok and McCanles did not have a good relationship, as McCanles often teased Hickok and Hickok began dating a woman named Sara Shull in whom McCanles was also interested.

In 1861, McCanles finally had enough and resolved to ambush Hickok at a train station with two accomplices. In the ensuing gunfight, McCanles and both his men were killed while Hickok emerged unscathed. Hickok managed to escape charges due to his claim of self-defense, and news of the shootout circulated throughout the country. It became known as the McCanles Massacre and started Hickok's reputation for being deadly with his pistols.

Wanting to escape the life of a gunfighter, Hickok traveled to Missouri where he enlisted in the Union Army as a wagon master and scout. It was during this time that Hickok would become friends with Custer (their friendship would be cut short after Custer's demise at Little Bighorn) and also earned his famous nickname, "Wild Bill."

In Missouri, Hickok came into conflict with a drunken mob who wanted to hang a bartender who had shot a criminal in an earlier incident. Hickok positioned himself between the crowd and the bartender, and when the crowd refused to back down, he drew his pistols and fired two shots over their heads. They quickly dispersed after that, and one of the women watching shouted out "Good for you, Wild Bill!"

This incident made the newspapers yet again, and James Hickok was officially branded as "Wild Bill" by the press. The name would stick with him for the rest of his life and beyond.

After the conclusion of the Civil War in 1865, Hickok was gambling in Springfield, Missouri. He lost a bet to a man named Dave Tutt. Hickok was unable to pay the money he lost, so Tutt confiscated Hickok's watch instead. Hickok requested that Tutt would not wear or display that watch in public as it would cause him humiliation. But Tutt was seen wearing it in public.

The watch was a prized possession of Hickok's and he challenged Tutt to a pistol duel the next day in the public square. Tutt, believing his own gunslinging skills were far superior to Hickock's, accepted the challenge.

The next morning, the two met in the public square of the town in front of a wide audience. Tutt proudly displayed the watch for everyone to see. After a tense moment, the two drew their pistols and fired. Hickok was unscathed, and Tutt fell dead to the ground from Hickok's bullet.

Many Western movies today often feature a quick-draw showdown in the streets of a frontier town between the primary protagonist and antagonist of the story. While these incidents were very rare in real life, the duel between Hickok and Tutt is an example of such a confrontation actually happening.

Hickok may have attempted to escape the life of a gunfighter, but his efforts were in vain. Many correspondents and journalists tracked down Hickok after hearing of his feats, and they embellished and exaggerated his exploits in their stories about him. These stories of Hickok circulated widely throughout the United States and gained a wide audience.

Wild Bill Hickok had become a national legend.

****

By this point, Hickok may have recognized that his skill with his revolvers and bravery in confronting dangerous people was his primary talent. He no longer attempted to pursue peaceful career paths as he had previously and decided to become a lawman.

He ran for sheriff of Ellsworth County in Kansas but lost in 1867. Hickok refused to give up. After another two-year stint in the army, he returned to Kansas again, this time to Hays City, where he ran for sheriff and emerged victorious.

Gunfights continued to be a part of Hickok's life. He shot and killed two men after being appointed sheriff of Hays City, and as with Hickok's previous gun battles, the stories of Wild Bill Hickok outdrawing and gunning down his opponents circulated in newspapers all over the country.

Hickok's tenure as Hays City Sheriff came to an end in 1870. His fame was so immense that many people wanted to kill him to gain their own fame and glory. As it would turn out, there were soldiers in the United States Army who wanted this as well.

In July 1870, Hickok was ambushed by several U.S. cavalry soldiers who beat him savagely. Despite being badly injured and attacked by multiple men at once, Hickok managed to draw and fire his Colt Navy revolvers in self-defense, killing one of the soldiers and wounding another while the others fled.

Hickok was forced to flee Hays City, eventually finding himself in Abilene. For the remainder of his life, Hickok remained on his guard against people trying to assassinate him so they would be known as "the one who killed Wild Bill Hickok."

In Abilene, Hickok was hired to become the Marshal. It was during his stint as Marshal that he encountered John Wesley Hardin, a gunfighter and outlaw who was on the run from law enforcement. Perhaps surprisingly, Hickok befriended Hardin rather than attempting to apprehend him, and the two gambled and drank together often. Hickok assured

Hardin that as long as he remained peaceful, he could stay and enjoy himself in Abilene.

But Hardin was not the type of man who could stay peaceful for long. While asleep at an Abilene hotel, Hardin was awakened by the sound of another tenant snoring in the next room. In a fit of rage, Hardin drew a revolver and fired two shots into the room.

Hickok was alerted by the gunfire and ran into the hotel with his revolvers drawn. Hardin spotted Hickok and escaped through the window to go to a haystack, where he remained hidden until dawn when he stole a horse and rode out of town.

****

Hickok didn't remain Marshal of Abilene much longer after that. Abilene's city council was growing increasingly annoyed that Hickok was dedicating less of his time to law enforcement and more of his time to gambling and womanizing. The fact that Hickok had allowed Hardin to escape didn't do him any favors either.

In 1871, Hickok had another violent confrontation, this time with Phil Coe and Ben Thompson, the owners of the most popular saloon in Abilene. Controversy erupted when Coe and Thompson purchased a painting of a Texas Longhorn bull with oversized genitalia for the saloon, deeply offending the townspeople.

Despite the protests of Coe and Thompson, Hickok sided with the townspeople and held them at gunpoint with a shotgun until the painting was altered to be more acceptable. Coe and Thompson sold the saloon shortly after, but the grudge against Hickok was firmly established.

Thompson left town while Coe stayed behind as a gambler and waited for the perfect moment to take on Hickok. Their feud escalated further when Hickok and Coe began dating the same woman. Many people in the town believed it was only a matter of time before Hickok and Coe would settle their dispute.

At the end of the cattle drive that year, Coe was drinking and celebrating with his friends in the saloon. During the celebrations, a dog attempted to bite Coe, who retaliated by drawing his revolver and firing at the animal.

Even though Coe missed the dog, the gunfire attracted the attention of Hickok who promptly entered the saloon with his Deputy Mike Williams. Hickok ordered the severely drunken Coe to surrender his gun, but instead, Coe decided to take advantage of the opportunity to kill Hickok.

Coe raised his revolver and fired a shot at Hickok that missed; Hickok drew his gun and shot Coe twice in the stomach. When Hickok heard footsteps behind him after gunning down Coe, he spun around and fired again, only to realize too late that he had shot Williams and killed him instantly.

The city council of Abilene finally had enough and dismissed Hickok as Marshal.

Hickok's life went on a downward spiral after his time in Abilene. Hickok reconnected with his old friend Buffalo Bill Cody and made good money as part of Cody's "Scouts of the Prairies," but he lost most of his money on gambling and sex workers.

By 1876, Hickok was balding, his eyesight was getting progressively worse (impeding his ability to shoot accurately), and he began to wear glasses. He reconnected with an old flame named Agnes Thatcher, and the two married in Wyoming before traveling to Ohio for their honeymoon and to settle down.

But Hickok was known as Wild Bill for a reason, and he came to realize that the quiet life with a wife was not for him. When the big news that gold had been discovered in Deadwood came to Ohio, it proved too tempting for Hickok to resist.

****

Hickok's reputation as a deadly gunfighter and gambler was in full force when he arrived in Deadwood. Hickok was a heavy drinker and acutely aware that, in his states of drunkenness, his alertness to and ability to detect people who could try to kill him were greatly reduced. His poorer eyesight wasn't doing him any favors either.

This is why Hickok always had a policy of sitting with his back against the wall so the entrance of the saloon was within his line of sight. That way, he could always see who was entering. But in Deadwood, he was taking an extra risk.

After arriving in Deadwood, Hickok fell back into his old life as a gambler, and he became a common presence in the saloons throughout the settlement. He was unable to hide his identity because he was so recognizable, and the news that Wild Bill was in Deadwood became the talk of the town.

In early August 1876, Hickok defeated a young man named Jack McCall at a poker table, completely cleaning him out. The humiliated McCall, who was already known for his temper, became infuriated. Hickok attempted to diffuse the situation by giving McCall enough money to buy a meal and advising him to never play poker again.

McCall didn't take Hickok's advice well and began repeatedly drunkenly boasting to others about how he was going to kill Hickok in revenge, but no one believed that McCall was serious.

The next day, Hickok entered a saloon but to his chagrin found that each of the available seats at the poker table had their back to the front entrance. Against his better instinct, Hickok violated his own rule and sat down at the table.

Drunk at the bar, McCall saw Hickok playing poker with his back turned to him. Seeing his opportunity, he made his move. Stumbling right up to Hickok's back, McCall drew his Colt Single Action Army .45 revolver and shouted, "Take that!" before shooting Hickok in the back of the head.

The bullet exited Hickok's cheek and struck another player at the table in the wrist. Hickok was killed instantly and slumped forward on the table in a growing pool of blood.

The hand that Hickok held, a pair of Aces and Eights each, became known as the Dead Man's Hand.

Hickok's luck had run out.

****

There are many reasons used to explain why Hickok's luck ran out that day. When he arrived in Deadwood, Hickok was simply no longer the alert and attentive man of his youth. He had aged significantly despite only being 39 years old and was further worn down from the heavy effects of the alcohol that he had consumed in great quantities throughout his life.

Most notably, Hickok had his back turned to the entrance of the saloon he died in, something he'd never done before. It is unknown if Hickok decided to take the risk believing he would be safe or if he simply no longer cared at that point.

McCall was somehow found not guilty at a hastily assembled court in Deadwood. He fled the town, only to be later tracked down, re-tried, and executed.

Wild Bill Hickok was buried in a cemetery outside of Deadwood, and an American flag was installed on his tombstone in remembrance of his service in the Civil War.

To this day, he remains one of the most iconic and larger-than-life figures of the Old West.

CALAMITY JANE

Despite being known for her daredevil nature, the frontierswoman Calamity Jane had a soft side to her as well. It also turned out that she was immune to smallpox, so when the deadly virus struck the mining town of Deadwood, Jane got to work treating the men, women, and children who became stricken with the disease. Her work saved many lives.

When Wild Bill Hickok arrived in Deadwood in 1876, he didn't arrive alone. Accompanying him was a woman whom he had met while enroute to the town, a woman who was perhaps even more wild than he was.

This woman's adopted name was Calamity Jane (actually Martha Jane Canary), and she was one of the most untamed real-life characters of the Old West. A woman who lived (and dressed) like a man, Calamity Jane could outshoot and outdrink most men she encountered in the saloons she frequented. She was also well-known for her wild, unpredictable, and often cantankerous nature.

The reason why she befriended Hickok on her way to Deadwood, perhaps, was because he was one of the few men, she met who could handle her outrageous personality.

But as we'll soon see, even though Calamity Jane was often one to raise hell by shooting first and asking questions later, she had a compassionate side to her as well.

****

Calamity Jane had a turbulent life well before she arrived in Deadwood. Born Martha Jane Canary in Missouri in 1852, the woman who would later become known as Calamity Jane was the oldest of six children.

From a young age, Martha Jane (who often just went by "Jane") had to learn how to care for her younger siblings, who consisted of two brothers and three sisters. Their father, Robert, had a serious gambling problem and often wasted the family's money, and their mother, Charlotte, seemed to have a difficult time keeping the household together between raising six children and dealing with her husband.

In 1865, the Canary family moved from Missouri to Virginia City in Montana Territory. Charlotte tragically passed away of pneumonia enroute. Robert, Jane, and Jane's five siblings managed to make it to Virginia City, where Robert abruptly decided to change plans and take the family to Salt Lake City in Utah instead.

Arriving there in the summer, Robert purchased 40 acres of land for farming purposes, but the following year tragedy struck again when Robert unexpectedly died. Just 14 years old, Jane found herself the new leader of the family and was forced to work the land just to provide a living for her younger siblings.

Jane, however, was unable to work the farm on her own. The next year, taking matters into her own hands, she loaded her brothers and sisters and their belongings into a wagon and took them to Fort Bridger in Wyoming Territory, before hopping on the Union Pacific Railroad to Piedmont.

Desperate to feed her siblings, Jane found out early on that it was incredibly difficult to find work as a young girl. With a tall height and masculine build, Jane decided to adopt a masculine persona and began wearing men's clothing to gain employment at places that would not hire women. She would continue wearing men's clothing for most of the rest of her life.

In the late 1860s and early 1870s, Jane worked a wide variety of jobs, including as an ox team driver, cook, dishwasher, and even as a sex worker. Jane had learned how to ride horses, navigate land, and hunt animals from her father Robert in her youth, which made her a natural fit to become a scout for the army despite being a woman.

She subsequently was able to find work as a scout at Fort Russell in Wyoming, and this took her with teams of U.S. cavalry into the Great Plains. Serving with the cavalry, Jane took part in battles with the hostile tribes they encountered and regularly scouted ahead, carried dispatches, and hunted game for the men to eat. This has never been validated by the Army and was told by Jane in her later stories about her life.

In 1873, Jane claimed that she was named "Calamity Jane" by her commander Captain Egan when she saved him from an Indian war party and successfully dragged him back to safety. Whether the story is true or not is unverified, but regardless, the name stuck with Jane for the rest of her life.

After a few years of serving with the cavalry on the plains, Jane returned to Fort Laramie in Wyoming. She became deathly ill from pneumonia, but she managed to pull through and survive despite being bedridden for weeks.

After her recovery, Jane found out about a wagon train that was heading north into Deadwood. Jane joined the train and befriended one of its occupants: Wild Bill Hickok.

Hickok and Jane hit it off almost immediately, although the true nature of their relationship remains uncertain to this day. Jane claimed in her later life that she and Hickok were romantic partners, though many other people who knew both of them at the time contradicted her claim. Regardless, it is clear that Hickok and Jane were, at the very least, very close friends and tight-knit by the time they arrived in Deadwood in June 1876.

Like Hickok, Jane had a penchant for drinking copious amounts of hard liquor, and the two of them spent much of their time gambling and getting severely drunk in Deadwood's saloons. Jane was nonetheless able to find work in Deadwood as a Pony Express rider by carrying mail between Deadwood and Custer, another town about 50 miles through the Black Hills Territory.

This was a dangerous mission, not only because of how rough the terrain was but also because of the presence of Indian warriors who were still engaged in hostilities with settlers and U.S. military forces. Nonetheless, Jane was able to successfully carry mail back and forth between Deadwood and Custer safely.

It was August 2 when Hickok was murdered at the gambling table by Jack McCall. Jane attempted to kill McCall with a meat cleaver (having left her firearms back at her residence), but she was stopped when McCall was apprehended by other residents of Deadwood instead.

Hickok's funeral was held the following day; nearly the entire population of Deadwood took part. Jane personally saw to it that Hickok's burial place stood out from the other graves in the cemetery by having it surrounded with a fence and an American flag posted to commemorate his service in the military.

Life was never quite the same for Jane in Deadwood after Hickok's passing. She continued to deliver mail between Custer and Deadwood, and in one notable incident, she took over a stagecoach when the driver was killed by Indians and drove it successfully while evading Indian arrows and gunfire all the way to Deadwood.

Two years later, in 1878, smallpox struck the famous Wild West town.

****

As a small frontier town essentially in the middle of nowhere, Deadwood had very little in the way of supplies or medicine. Furthermore, most of the doctors in the town were poorly trained and medical equipment was scarce. The only real medicine to treat pain that was on hand was calomel (which could help relieve pain but would destroy gums and teeth in the process) and a variety of alcohol and narcotics.

As a result, once it arrived, the people could do virtually nothing to stop smallpox from overtaking the town. When the epidemic was in full force, the people created a quarantine area where the sick and dying were housed. Men, women, and children alike were afflicted.

Jane, however, was one of the few people in Deadwood who was immune to the disease. When the disease struck, she immediately stopped drinking and gambling and got to work nursing and caring for the sick.

One witness referred to the usually irascible Jane as "a perfect angel sent from heaven when any of the boys was sick."

What's more, Jane abstained from her unpredictable behavior and drinking habits throughout the entire epidemic. She used her own money to pay for food for the sick, went out into the forest to collect fresh water for them from the creek, and worked all day and night caring for them.

Even though Jane had a grumpy and wild personality, during the smallpox epidemic in Deadwood, she displayed incredible compassion for the afflicted.

It is believed that dozens of people who came down with smallpox in Deadwood survived because of Calamity Jane's tireless efforts to care for them and ensure their survival. Many nursing organizations to this day acknowledge Calamity Jane's honorable actions and argue that she set a model for providing consistent and exceptional care regardless of the circumstances - one that nurses today should try to emulate.

****

Unfortunately, Calamity Jane returned to her vices and hard-living lifestyle after the smallpox outbreak had passed.

She traveled throughout the American West finding employment in a variety of places (including in Buffalo Bill's Wild West Show), and she returned to Deadwood for a final time in the summer of 1903.

Poor from having spent all her money on alcohol, Jane's addiction was bearing down on her both physically and mentally by this point. Though she managed to find work at a brothel, cooking and doing laundry, her health problems continued to get worse.

Calamity Jane passed away on August 1, 1903. The funeral in Deadwood was the largest at the time ever held for a woman, and the man who closed her coffin was someone she had nursed back to health when he was a boy during the smallpox epidemic.

Calamity Jane was buried at Mount Moriah Cemetery, South Dakota, next to Bill Hickok. Four of the men who planned her funeral later stated that Hickok had "absolutely no use" for Jane while he was alive, so they decided to play a posthumous joke on him by burying her by his side. Another account states: "in compliance with Jane's dying requests, the Society of Black Hills Pioneers took charge of her funeral and burial in Mount Moriah Cemetery beside Wild Bill.

She was then laid to rest next to Wild Bill Hickok.

THE LINCOLN
COUNTY WAR

One of the biggest range wars of the Old West, the Lincoln County War, occurred in New Mexico in 1878. The war involved some of the famous figures of the Old West, including John Chisum, Billy the Kid, and the Regulators Gang. This chapter covers the major players of the Lincoln County War and what exactly went down.

Deadwood was not the only place in the Old West where murder and lawlessness were rife and where people often had to take the law into their own hands.

One year after the assassination of Wild Bill Hickok, tensions between rival factions were brewing to a boiling point down in Lincoln County, New Mexico Territory.

Whereas Deadwood was a rather small settlement of miners nestled in the mountains, Lincoln County was a vast landscape of plains and valleys controlled by powerful cattle barons. The conflict between these barons would soon erupt into an all-out range war (later named the Lincoln County War) that would be marked by murders and killings on a massive scale unlike anything seen elsewhere in the Old West.

Some of the most famous figures of the Old West, including John Tunstall, John Chisum, Patrick Garrett, and the infamous Billy the Kid, would take part in this war.

****

Lincoln County was the largest county in the United States at the time and occupied over one-fifth of New Mexico alone.

In the early 1870s, the only store in Lincoln County was owned by the wealthy Lawrence Murphy (one of the major cattle barons in the area) and his associate James Dolan. The store was appropriately named Murphy & Dolan Mercantile and Bank.

Since they owned the only store and bank in Lincoln County, Murphy and Dolan were able to monopolize the selling and trading of basic goods throughout Lincoln, making massive profits in the process. Virtually the entire economy of Lincoln County was controlled by these two men alone. Murphy and Dolan were also the primary suppliers of beef to the United States Army in New Mexico, which provided them with their primary source of income.

Furthermore, Murphy and Dolan also controlled the local sheriff (William Brady) and deputies of Lincoln County to ensure the law would always be on their side. Together, Murphy and Dolan and their allies were called "The House" by the local residents.

In essence, Murphy and Dolan were able to secure a tight grip over Lincoln by controlling both the county's economy and the legal system. Wielding their vast influence, they forced the smaller ranchers and farmers in the county to pay high prices for their goods, while also paying low prices for the farmers' crops and the ranchers' cattle.

Naturally, this made them enemies of many of the other ranchers and farmers in the county.

Murphy and Dolan's grip over Lincoln County, however, began to slip in the year 1877. A lawyer named Alexander "Alex" McSween and a young wealthy English banker named John Tunstall arrived in Lincoln County to compete directly with Murphy and Dolan.

They opened up a new business called H.H. Tunstall & Company almost directly next door to Murphy & Dolan Mercantile and Banking. In support of McSween and Tunstall was John Chisum, a wealthy cattle baron who was Murphy's only main rival in Lincoln. Chisum supported McSween and Tunstall because he saw an opportunity to break the economic and political power that Murphy and Dolan wielded.

One of Tunstall's hired guns was a young man who was good with a revolver named Henry McCarty. McCarty was a protege of Tunstall and would later say how he considered Tunstall to be the only good man he ever knew.

Murphy and Dolan recognized the threat that Chisum, McSween, and Tunstall collectively posed to them and began to plan countermeasures. This was what started the tensions that would eventually erupt into an all-out war.

As the dispute escalated, the local residents of Lincoln County were divided mainly along ethnic and religious lines. The Irish Catholics in the area sided with the Murphy-Dolan faction, as Murphy himself was an Irish immigrant who had come to the United States.

Meanwhile, the local English Protestants primarily sided with the Chisum-McSween-Tunstall faction.

****

Years earlier, Murphy and Dolan's business partner Emil Fritz had passed away. McSween collected the money disbursed from Fritz's insurance policy because he was the lawyer hired by the local estate.

McSween, however, refused to give the money to the estate executor because he believed the money would then be handed off to Murphy and Dolan. As a business competitor to Murphy and Dolan, McSween was naturally resistant to handing them a vast sum of cash.

This provided Murphy and Dolan with the excuse they needed to escalate the situation with their rivals. They obtained a court order to seize Tunstall and McSween's assets, with Sheriff Brady forming a posse to seize Tunstall's horses in particular.

Tunstall was delivering his horses back to Lincoln when he was discovered by Brady's posse. No one knows exactly what happened next, but there was a violent episode that ended with Tunstall being shot in the head and his horses taken.

Tunstall's murder was the event that officially set off the Lincoln County War as both factions now turned to the gun rather than the pen to fight each other. Murphy and Dolan hired gangs of cattle rustlers led by Jesse Evans to harass Chisum and Tunstall, launching numerous ambushes of Chisum's men and seizing his cattle.

McCarty was deeply affected by the murder of Tunstall. Seeking revenge against Murphy and Dolan, he formed a vigilante gang known as The Regulators that had the sole goal of bringing justice to Murphy and Dolan and their allies.

Consisting of 12 men at its peak, the Regulators were deputized by John Wilson, the Lincoln County Justice of the Peace, and set out to capture or kill Brady and his posse members.

Both sides in the war were now claiming to have the law on their side: Murphy and Dolan had Sheriff Brady and his deputies, and Chisum and McSween had the Regulators.

The Regulators went on a rampage throughout Lincoln County, seeking out each member of Brady's posse individually and either capturing or murdering them in cold blood, including Jesse Evans. Some in Lincoln County condemned the Regulators for their violent actions, as they were known for brutally shooting their opponents numerous times to ensure their deaths, while others viewed them as doing the right thing by taking vengeance against Tunstall's murderers.

Realizing that the tide was now turning against them, Murphy and Dolan turned to New Mexico Territory's Governor, Samuel Axtell, to side with them and un-deputize the Regulators. Axtell made the announcement that the Regulators had been illegally deputized and issued warrants for their arrests. Axtell also revoked law enforcement status for all law enforcement officers in Lincoln County other than Brady and his men.

The Governor's decree did nothing to hinder the Regulators. In early April 1878, the Regulators arrived in secret in Lincoln town. When Brady appeared on the street, they ambushed him and shot both him and several of his deputies dozens of times before speeding away in their horses and evading capture.

****

The Regulators' luck wouldn't last for much longer. McCarty and the Regulators met with Chisum and demanded a large sum of money for their work in fighting back against Murphy and Dolan. Chisum refused because he disapproved of the Regulators' murderous ways and believed they weren't any better than Murphy and Dolan.

The Regulators turned against Chisum and began stealing his horses in retaliation. By this point, the Regulators were essentially their own vigilante faction fighting against both Chisum/McSween and Murphy/Dolan, and the two factions in the war had suddenly become three.

Even though gunning down Brady was a major victory for them, the Regulators encountered a much tougher opponent in the form of Buckshot Roberts, a man who they believed had taken part in Tunstall's murder. When the Regulators attempted to ambush and kill Roberts, he managed to evade their gunfire and kill one of the Regulators while wounding four others.

Meanwhile, Murphy and Dolan formed a new posse to set out and eliminate the Regulators. In an ensuing shootout, three more Regulators were killed or captured, dwindling their numbers further.

The surviving Regulators, who called themselves the "Ironclad," returned to Lincoln in secret to meet with McSween at his store. They were discovered by Murphy and Dolan's men, who promptly surrounded the McSween store with the Regulators, McSween, and McSween's wife Susan trapped inside, along with several other women and children.

Murphy and Dolan's men lay siege to the store, with gunfire being exchanged over the next three days and several men on both sides being killed or wounded. Murphy and Dolan demanded the complete surrender of the Regulators, who each refused and responded with bullets.

Finally, U.S. Army soldiers commanded by Colonel Nathan Dudley arrived on the scene to help end the hostilities, only to be fired upon by the Regulators as well. In response, Dudley ordered cannons to be aimed at the McSween store.

McSween called out that he wanted to step out and negotiate with Murphy and Dolan, who refused and demanded his complete surrender. When McSween stepped out anyway, he was gunned down in cold blood.

The Regulators realized that their position was hopeless and knew they only had two options: surrender or attempt to shoot their way out. They chose the latter.

In one of the most incredible (and improbable) gun battles of the Old West, McCarty and the other Regulators burst out of the building with guns blazing and ran to their horses. Despite being completely outnumbered, surrounded, and fired upon from all sides by dozens of men, most of the Regulators including McCarty were able to jump on nearby horses and ride away out of town completely unscathed.

****

By this point, the Lincoln County War had attracted the attention of Washington D.C.

President Rutherford Hayes removed Axtell from the Governor's office and appointed Lew Wallace in his place. Hayes ordered Wallace to restore peace to Lincoln County.

Seeking the most peaceful solution possible, Wallace announced in November 1878 that amnesty would be granted to everyone on both sides in the Lincoln County War provided they were not already under indictment; with the only exception being McCarty, upon whom he imposed a $500 bounty.

Wallace's action effectively brought the Lincoln County War to a halt, with neither side victorious.

Murphy passed away from cancer a month before Wallace's announcement, and Dolan was granted possession over

Tunstall's property. Susan McSween filed charges against Dolan in an attempt to stop this, but he was acquitted.

Nonetheless, Susan was able to use the vast sums of money her husband and Tunstall had acquired before and during the war to purchase a ranch in Three Rivers, New Mexico, which later became one of the largest and most successful ranches in the country. She passed away in 1931 at the age of 85 as a very prosperous woman.

Chisum was left weakened by the war. He only had a fraction of the tens of thousands of heads of cattle he possessed before the conflict had broken out, but he still had an estate worth half a million dollars, an enormous sum at the time. Later finding out he was afflicted with cancer, he traveled back east to see his family in Arkansas and Texas before passing away in 1884.

Meanwhile, McCarty went on the run as a fugitive, committing more crimes and gaining the name "Billy the Kid."

BILLY THE KID

In 1881, the famous outlaw Henry McCarty, alias William H. Bonney, better known as Billy the Kid, *was tracked down and killed by his old friend Pat Garrett. But was McCarty really killed that day? There are and are rumors that "the Kid" survived that fateful encounter with Garrett. This chapter analyzes those rumors along with the events leading up to the McCarty and Garrett confrontation.*

Just 19 years old when he went on the run after his time with the Regulators in the Lincoln County War, Henry McCarty was one of the most wanted outlaws in America.

The new Governor of New Mexico Territory, Lew Wallace, had granted amnesty to all participants in the Lincoln County War except McCarty and placed a large bounty of $500 on his head.

This made McCarty an appealing target for everyone from law enforcement officers to bounty hunters to anyone else seeking the glory of killing or capturing "Billy the Kid."

McCarty was also extremely lucky. Throughout his time with the Regulators, he had found himself involved in or initiated several intense close-range gunfights and had emerged from each one without getting shot once.

His escape from Lincoln in particular was nothing short of miraculous. Despite dozens of men, including trained army soldiers, all opening fire on him from many directions when he burst out of McSween's store with two guns blazing, McCarty still managed to make it onto a horse and speed away without so much as a scratch.

The stories from these incidents gained national attention and greatly increased McCarty's fame and notoriety. Throughout the late 1870s and into the early 1880s, he traveled throughout the American Southwest with other outlaws, committing robberies and rustling cattle with possies of law enforcement officers and bounty hunters continuously in hot pursuit.

For how much longer would McCarty's luck last?

****

Henry McCarty was born on September 17, 1859, in New York City, to Patrick and Katherine McCarty.

Patrick passed away almost directly after the conclusion of the Civil War, and Katherine moved McCarty and his brother Joseph westward to Indiana and then to Kansas. In 1870, Katherine was diagnosed with tuberculosis and was instructed by her doctors to move to a drier climate. Katherine then took her sons south to the deserts of New Mexico, where she married a bartender named William Antrim in 1873.

The new family didn't stay together for long. Antrim abandoned the family less than a year later to search for gold, and Katherine was forced to rent out rooms in the family's home to make ends meet. Unfortunately, Katherine's condition worsened until she passed away in late 1874, making McCarty an orphan at 14 years old.

The owner of a local boarding house, Sarah Brown, was sympathetic to McCarty and offered him food to eat and a room to sleep in exchange for work. It didn't take long, however, for McCarty to turn to the life of a criminal.

In McCarty's first known criminal act aged only 16 years, he was caught stealing food, and no less than ten days later, he and a friend were caught stealing clothing and firearms from a Chinese laundry. McCarty was found guilty and jailed, but he managed to escape two days later. Becoming caught and imprisoned only to escape his jail cell would become a recurring theme throughout McCarty's short life.

Now on the run from the law and not knowing where to go, McCarty traveled to meet Antrim. His stepfather, however, did not treat him warmly, so McCarty returned the favor by taking Antrim's clothes and guns when he was away from home. Then he went on the run again.

Traveling to Arizona Territory, McCarty found work as a ranch hand, but he gambled most of his money away in the local saloons. Desperate for cash, McCarty turned to his criminal ways yet again. He met and became friends with Scottish criminal and former Cavalry soldier John Mackie. Working together, the two stole numerous horses from the US Army and resold them to make money.

Around this time, McCarty began referring to himself as William "Billy" Bonney as an alias to help cover his true identity.

McCarty committed his first killing in 1877. He was at a saloon in Bonita, Arizona, when he found himself in an altercation with a blacksmith named Francis Cahill. Tensions between McCarty and Cahill had been building as the two had been name-calling and insulting each other for weeks.

The conflict between the two reached a boiling point in the Bonita saloon and the much larger Cahill threw McCarty to the floor and began to beat him. McCarty drew his revolver and shot and mortally wounded Cahill, who passed away the following day. McCarty was captured by the local Justice of the Peace, but he escaped before law enforcement officers could arrive.

Now a wanted man in Arizona, McCarty returned to New Mexico Territory. He was ambushed by Apache warriors along the way, who stole his horse and all his belongings. McCarty walked on foot to Fort Stanton and was only barely alive from starvation and dehydration when he stumbled into the home of his friend John Jones, whose family nursed him back to health over the subsequent weeks.

After making a full recovery, McCarty traveled to Lincoln County and met British businessman John Tunstall, who was working with Alexander McSween and John Chisum to compete against the economic empire run by Lawrence Murphy and James Dolan as discussed in the previous chapter.

Tunstall took a liking to the young McCarty and hired him to help guard his cattle. Tunstall also treated McCarty very well and respectfully, earning McCarty's friendship and loyalty. McCarty would later say that Tunstall was the only man who had ever treated him decently.

It appeared that McCarty's life was on the upswing and that he could at long last leave his criminal career behind him.

Unfortunately, that would not turn out to be the case. Tunstall's shooting and murder at the hands of Murphy and Dolan's men in 1878 had a major psychological and emotional impact on McCarty and marked the most significant turning point in his life since the passing of his mother.

McCarty vowed revenge against Tunstall's murderers and joined the Regulators gang to exact justice against the Murphy and Dolan faction.

****

When the Lincoln County War had concluded about a year later, McCarty had become one of the most wanted outlaws in the country and Governor Wallace had put a large bounty on his head.

McCarty, by now known as "Billy the Kid," was continuously on the run and joining other criminals to rob local ranchers of their horses. The bounty hunters and law enforcement officers who went after him were unable to catch up to him. McCarty simply had a knack for evading the men who were sent to capture or kill him.

By 1879, Governor Wallace decided to change course after efforts to apprehend "the Kid" had continuously failed. He heard rumors that McCarty would be willing to surrender in exchange for amnesty if he testified against other men who had committed crimes during the Lincoln County War. Wallace sent a message to McCarty that he wanted to meet privately with him to discuss it.

Sure enough, McCarty showed up to meet with Wallace (albeit with a Winchester rifle in one hand and a Colt revolver in the other). Wallace had a very generous offer for McCarty: McCarty would submit to a public arrest and be locked up in jail until the day of his testimony. If he could indict other men involved in the Lincoln County War at his trial, he would then be set free. McCarty agreed.

Everything went according to plan, and at McCarty's trial, he helped to indict Dolan with his testimony.

McCarty expected to be set free per his agreement with Wallace, but the local district attorney (who disagreed with

Wallace's decision) defied the Governor's order and locked him up again.

True to form, McCarty wouldn't remain a prisoner for long. When the law enforcement officers returned to his jail cell one-morning several weeks later to check on him, his cell was open and empty. Perhaps purely because of talent, McCarty was simply a master escape artist who could evade each posse sent after him and break out of jail cells when he was captured.

McCarty formed a new gang, this one called the Rustlers, that consisted of Billy Wilson, Tom O'Folliard, Tom Pickett, Charlie Bowdre, and Dave Rudabaugh. Some of these men had previously served with McCarty in the Regulators gang.

Together, the newly-formed Rustlers began stealing horses and cattle throughout Lincoln County. Newspapers began circulating with headlines dubbing Billy the Kid as "the most important outlaw" in New Mexico Territory.

In early 1880, a man named Joe Grant arrived in New Mexico seeking to find and kill McCarty. Grant made no secret publicly of his personal mission, and McCarty was able to find out via the press.

McCarty learned where Grant was and walked right up to him in a saloon. Grant didn't know what McCarty looked like, so McCarty played to Grant's ego and pretended to be an admirer of him. During their back-and-forth banter, Grant showed off his Colt Peacemaker revolver that he said he would "kill Billy the Kid with."

He handed the revolver to McCarty, who secretly removed three cartridges from the cylinder before handing it back to the distracted Grant.

McCarty then announced to Grant that he was Billy the Kid. Shocked, Grant tried to shoot McCarty at close range three times, but each time the hammer fell over an empty chamber. After the third failed shot, McCarty drew his own revolver and shot Grant directly in the head, killing him instantly.

The news that "Billy the Kid" was involved in another shooting gained national attention and Governor Wallace put the $500 bounty on McCarty's head yet again.

****

The Sheriff of Lincoln County, Patrick "Pat" Garrett, set out to find and apprehend McCarty following the shooting of Joe Grant.

Garrett was a former buffalo hunter who had come to New Mexico Territory in search of a new life. He found work as a ranch hand and as a bartender in Lincoln, and it was here that he had met McCarty who was working for John Tunstall at the time.

Garrett and McCarty would spend lots of time together working cattle and drinking in the bars. They became very good friends, with people who knew the two reporting that Garrett called McCarty "Little Casino" and McCarty called Garrett "Big Casino."

But now Garrett would have to set out to capture or kill the young man who had been his very good friend. Forming a posse of deputies, Garrett planned to ambush McCarty at Fort Sumner, having received a tip that the Rustlers gang would be there.

When McCarty rode in with the rest of the Rustlers gang, Garrett and his deputies opened fire. They managed to kill one of the gang, (O'Folliard), but McCarty and the rest escaped.

Again, McCarty was extremely lucky, as it was hardly the first time that multiple men had opened fire on him, and yet again he managed to ride away without getting hit.

Garrett was undeterred by his failure to kill McCarty and continued to relentlessly pursue the Rustlers gang for the next few months. Finally, Garrett and his deputies were able to catch the Rustlers gang by surprise and surround them at a place called Stinking Springs. All members of the gang, including McCarty, surrendered and were transported in shackles to Las Vegas, New Mexico.

In Las Vegas, the prisoners were loaded onto a train to be taken to Santa Fe for trial. An armed mob gathered outside of the train and demanded that Garrett surrender Dave Rudabaugh, who they wanted for the murder of a deputy he had committed the prior year. Garrett refused to surrender Rudabaugh, leading to a tense standoff until Garrett agreed to allow some of the members of the mob onto the train where they could personally petition the Governor to hand Rudabaugh to them.

Throughout the whole incident, McCarty remained very calm. Witnesses who were on the train with him reported how he verbally expressed his desire to shoot everyone in the crowd with his Winchester rifle.

At his new trial in April 1881, McCarty was found guilty of murder and sentenced to hang. Legend has it that when the judge pronounced the sentence, he told McCarty that he would hang until he was "dead, dead, dead" to which McCarty retorted that the judge could go to "hell, hell, hell."

McCarty was transported again to Lincoln where he was held prisoner on the top floor of the courthouse. But he wouldn't remain a prisoner for long. Strategically choosing a day when most of the law enforcement officers of the courthouse were away on other duties and errands, McCarty feigned that he needed to use the bathroom.

A deputy transported McCarty over to the outhouse. On their way back into the courthouse, while the two were walking up the stairs, McCarty suddenly broke free of the deputy and ran up the stairs and hid around the corner, where he managed to slip out of his handcuffs. When the deputy came around the corner, McCarty beat him savagely with the cuffs and took his revolver before shooting him dead.

With his legs still shackled, McCarty shuffled his way into Garrett's office and took his double-barreled shotgun. He then moved to the window, called out for the other deputy to appear, and shot him dead too. He then grabbed an ax to break the shackles around his ankles, before running outside, jumping on a horse, and riding out of the town. Witnesses claimed that McCarty was singing as he rode out.

****

That was the last time that McCarty would be so lucky.

Garrett rode to Fort Sumner with two more deputies in the summer of 1881 to the home of cattle baron Lucien Maxwell. Lucien was the father of Peter Maxwell, a known friend of McCarty's.

Garrett met with Lucien and revealed his plan to ambush McCarty when he inevitably arrived to meet with Peter; Lucien agreed.

What happened next is disputed, but the basic sequence of events goes like this: McCarty came to the Maxwell house that night when it was very dark inside. Garrett and his deputies were hidden inside the house with their revolvers drawn.

McCarty entered the home looking for something to eat, while Garrett remained hidden in the shadows. Due to the poor lighting, Garrett was initially unable to verify if the man who had just entered the home was, in fact, McCarty.

McCarty suddenly grew suspicious when he heard a noise in the dark from Garrett and drew his revolver, shouting out, "*Quien es? Quien es?*"

Recognizing McCarty's voice, Garrett aimed his revolver at McCarty and fired twice. One of the bullets missed, but the other struck McCarty just under his heart. McCarty collapsed to the ground and was dead within a matter of minutes.

The body was later examined by the local coroner's jury of six people, who confirmed that the body was McCarty's. The body was given a candlelight wake and buried the next day, and newspapers all over the country reported how the infamous Billy the Kid had finally met his end.

That was the end of Billy the Kid…or was it?

****

Was Billy the Kid really killed that day? Legends and rumors grew in the years immediately following the shooting that the entire event had been staged by Garrett and that the body buried was not McCarty's.

Garrett's personal friendship with McCarty had never died away, the rumors said, and the two arranged for Garrett to "shoot" McCarty when in reality McCarty would slip away to evade the law and live a peaceful life with a new identity. These rumors continued for decades.

Many people, most notably Brushy Bill Roberts of Texas and John Miller of Arizona came forward to claim that they were McCarty. But their stories could neither be proven nor disproven, and all later DNA tests conducted using Miller's remains were found to be inconclusive.

Whether Henry McCarty was shot and killed by Garrett that night or went on to live a quiet life with a new name remains a mystery to this day. Regardless, what's not a mystery is that Billy the Kid's reign of terror had finally come to an end.

GUNFIGHT AT
THE O.K. CORRAL

In October 1881, the most famous gunfight in Western history occurred in Tombstone, Arizona. The Earp Brothers (Wyatt, Virgil, and Morgan) and Doc Holliday took on the Cowboys, consisting of the Clanton brothers, McLaury brothers, and Billy Claiborne. This chapter covers the events leading up to the famous gunfight and its immediate aftermath.

Even those who don't know Old West history have likely heard of the gunfight at the O.K. Corral.

This gunfight, which undoubtedly became the most well-known shootout of the Old West, has been the subject of countless films including *My Darling Clementine, Gunfight at the O.K. Corral*, *Tombstone,* and *Wyatt Earp*, among many others.

Names like Wyatt Earp and Doc Holliday have become immortalized as well. Most films depict Earp as the archetype of the stoic Frontier Marshal who enforces law and order, and Holliday as his often drunk and yet loyal friend who spends a lot of his time in the saloon and is fast with his six guns. In reality, the real Wyatt Earp and Doc Holliday were far more complex people than what Western movies often like to depict.

The reason why the story of O.K. Corral has been told and retold in the media, and embedded in the collective minds of the general public, is not because of the gunfight itself. The actual shootout was shorter and more sickening — and less epic and grandiose — than what you usually see in Hollywood and only lasted thirty seconds.

Rather, the real reason why the O.K. Corral gained so much attention is that it represented the major turning point in the conflict between the Earp brothers and the Cowboy gang.

As we'll soon see, the growing feud between these two parties that led up to the O.K. Corral gunfight and the significant (and bloody) ramifications that resulted from it form the real story.

****

In 1877, silver was discovered in Cochise County, Arizona Territory.

Just as thousands of people had flocked to the badlands of South Dakota when gold was discovered there a couple of years prior, now people raced to the deserts of Arizona, coalescing around a settlement that would become known as Tombstone.

Between 1879 and 1881, Tombstone transformed from a small prospecting settlement of a few tents into a full-blown boomtown of over 10,000 people, complete with hotels, saloons, brothels, homes, and a rapidly shaping political system.

Tombstone was not exactly a town known for its peacefulness. South Dakota had Deadwood as its settlement of lawlessness and anarchy, and Arizona had Tombstone. Murder, shootings, cattle rustling, robberies, sex work, gambling, and drunkenness were all rife in and around this desert frontier town, which was only 30 miles away from the Mexican border. People came to Tombstone to either make a fortune or die trying.

By 1881, the social and political culture of the town had clearly divided across two lines: the "Cowboys' faction and the "Earp" faction and their respective allies.

The Cowboys faction was a loosely organized group of outlaws, which included members such as Curly Bill Brocius (who was not at the shootout), Ike Clanton, Billy Claiborne, and the McLaury brothers (Tom and Frank). The Cowboys were outlaws, bandits, thieves, and desperados who were known for committing robberies and crimes throughout Cochise County. By 1880, legitimate cowboys, cattlemen, and ranchers in the area were taking offense to be called a "Cowboy."

The Earp brothers, consisting of Virgil, Wyatt, and Morgan, had arrived in Tombstone in 1879. The Earps were known for being extremely close-knit and had worked together as saloon owners, pimps, and lawmen in several frontier towns throughout their careers. Even though the brothers had arrived in Tombstone to pursue ventures other than police work, Virgil and Wyatt in particular had built reputations as tough-as-nails lawmen, and their arrival in lawless Tombstone naturally created appreciation or apprehension (depending on who you asked) among the town's residents.

The Earps soon found that they would be unable to leave their law enforcement careers behind. Virgil, who arrived days before Wyatt and Morgan, was convinced by the Pima

County Marshal to be named Deputy Marshal on account of his many years of experience. Less than a year later, he would also be named the acting Marshal of Tombstone following the shooting of Marshal Frank White at the hands of Curly Bill Brocius.

Six weeks after White's death, Virgil ran for the position of Town Marshal but was defeated in the election by Ben Sippy. Virgil, however, became Marshal anyway when it was discovered that Sippy had financial irregularities in his records. This meant that Virgil would be both the Deputy U.S. Marshal and the Town Marshal by the time of the O.K. Corral gunfight.

Wyatt Earp would become the most well-known of the Earp brothers. Wyatt was younger than Virgil and had less law enforcement experience at the time the brothers arrived in Tombstone, but he was no less intimidating. Wyatt was noted for his strong build, and his history as a boxer meant he knew how to handle himself with his fists.

Wyatt was also known for being good with his pistol and had developed a reputation as a strong, no-nonsense law enforcement officer who wasn't afraid to pistol whip those disturbing the peace, most notably while he was serving as a Marshal in Dodge City. Besides his law enforcement and boxing experience, Wyatt also had much experience as a buffalo hunter.

Morgan, the younger brother, had served as a law enforcement officer in Montana but had no experience in a gunfight. Morgan had, however, assisted Virgil with his law enforcement duties.

A good friend of Wyatt was John "Doc" Holliday, a Georgia-born dentist turned gambler who was also known for being good with a pistol. Holliday had met Wyatt in 1878, and Wyatt claimed that Holliday had saved his life at one time. However, Holliday was also known for his sometimes-uncontrollable temper that could flare up when he turned to liquor, and he also suffered from tuberculosis.

Holliday had arrived in Arizona officially because the drier climate was supposed to help the effects of his condition, and also because he decided to follow the Earps there.

****

Tensions between the Cowboys and the Earps began to grow in 1880. The two sides were opposed to each other on both economic and political grounds as well as personal feuds that had developed between the factions. The Cowboys, who were headed by the McLaury and Clanton families, were predominantly Texan Democrats and were supported by many rural ranchers in the area. The Cowboys were also backed up by the Sheriff of Cochise County, Johnny Behan.

The faction led by the Earps, meanwhile, were primarily Republicans and businessmen who operated within Tombstone's city limits and were backed by several of the wealthy businessmen in the county.

In late October of that year, Marshal Fred White attempted to disarm some of the Cowboys who were firing their revolvers into the air late at night.

No one knows exactly what happened next, except that when White specifically tried to disarm Curly Bill Brocius, the gun went off and the bullet struck White in the abdomen. White would die of his wounds a few days later.

Some people claim that Curly Bill's gun went off because he was drunk, while others claim that he had deliberately murdered White. Regardless, after the shot that killed White was fired, Wyatt appeared and pistol-whipped Curly Bill before arresting him, despite the protests of the Cowboys who were there.

Curly Bill managed to avoid being convicted because it was decided that the evidence more strongly suggested the shooting was accidental. Nonetheless, the shooting of White and Wyatt's arrest of Curly Bill only exacerbated the agitation between the Earps and the Cowboys further.

Wyatt also had a professional (and later personal) rivalry with Behan. Earlier, both men had run for the position of Cochise County Sheriff. However, Behan managed to convince Wyatt to drop out of the race by promising him the position of undersheriff. When Behan was appointed the position by the governor and legislature, he reneged on his deal and appointed another man to the undersheriff position. Behan claimed that he reneged on the deal because Wyatt had threatened Ike Clanton, a member of the Cowboy gang, in Behan's name.

The rivalry between Wyatt and Behan became personal when Wyatt developed a relationship with Behan's common-law wife, Josephine "Sadie" Marcus. Josephine had ended her relationship with Behan after discovering his infidelities.

The quarrel between the Earps and the Cowboys grew further heated in October 1881 when a Tombstone ordinance was passed that prohibited the carrying of firearms within city limits. This infuriated the Cowboys gang, who enjoyed being able to carry their rifles and pistols wherever they went. Virgil was responsible for enforcing this law, and this drew the ire of the Cowboys further when he forced them to surrender their weapons when they visited town.

A heated altercation took place between Doc Holliday and Ike Clanton, who were both drunk, at the end of October in the Alhambra saloon. Although the fight was broken up, Clanton continued making violent threats against Holliday and the Earps and drank into the morning. Virgil then arrived and disarmed the severely drunk Clanton of his weapons before taking him to the judge.

The judge, however, only imposed a fine on Clanton and allowed his guns to be returned to him. Even though the judge was lenient, Ike and the Cowboys had had enough.

Clanton left town and returned with four more Cowboys: his brother Billy Clanton, Billy Claiborne, and the McLaury brothers Frank and Tom. The five men paraded themselves around Tombstone with their revolvers holstered on their gun belts and announced that they would not surrender their weapons this time.

The Earps realized that the time had come to confront the Cowboys. Virgil, Wyatt, Morgan, and Holliday assembled in the streets of Tombstone. The four planned only to disarm the Cowboys without violence, but they were acutely aware that violence was a very real probability.

This is why each man made sure to arm himself before walking down to the O.K. Corral. Each of the four carried a revolver, and Virgil had a double-barreled shotgun that he passed off to Holliday, who hid the weapon under his long coat.

The four then marched down the street to confront the Cowboys. Behan met them approximately halfway and claimed that he had already disarmed them, but the four pressed on anyway.

The stage was now set. The gunfight at the O.K. Corral was about to begin.

****

The gunfight at the O.K. Corral, which actually took place about six doors west of the soon-to-be-famous horse corral, was over almost as fast as it started.

When the Earps and Holliday came around the corner to confront the Cowboys, the two groups of men were only about six to ten feet apart from one another.

There was a tense moment, and Virgil said something to the effect of ordering the Cowboys to put up their hands and turn over their guns. Instead, Frank McLaury and Billy Clanton dropped their hands to their holstered revolvers at their gun belts, at which point the Earps dropped their hands to their revolvers that were kept in the pockets of their long coats.

"No, I don't want that!" Virgil said.

A few seconds went by without a word as both sides stared each other down with their hands over their revolvers.

No one knows who drew and fired first, but by the end of the gunfight, it was clear what had happened:

Thirty shots were fired in roughly 30 seconds; Ike Clanton and Billy Claiborne ran away from the fight; the McLaury brothers and Billy Clanton were each shot multiple times and killed; Virgil was shot in the leg and wounded; Morgan was shot across the back and wounded; Holliday was grazed with a bullet in the leg; and Wyatt miraculously emerged from the quick and close-range shootout completely unscathed.

News of what happened near the O.K. Corral quickly spread across the country. It eventually became one of the most famous gunfights of the Old West, if not the most famous. It was known as the shootout where the Earps took on and triumphed over the Cowboys in a gunfight and numerous legends and myths about what happened proliferated across America and remain to this day.

Modern-day legend and Hollywood get a lot wrong about the O.K. Corral, however. Most older films made about the gunfight in particular depict it as the climax to the feud between the Earps and the Cowboy gang, when (as we'll soon see in the upcoming chapters) the truth was the gunfight only exacerbated the feud and overshadowed the sequence of violent events that would come after.

Additionally, many films involving the OK Corral romanticize it as much more glorious than it actually was. Movies routinely show the Earps and Cowboys much farther apart from one another than they were and depict the gunfight going on a lot longer than 30 seconds, for instance, and often fail to capture the true intensity and gruesome aspects of the fight.

In reality, the gunfight at the O.K. Corral was very brief, intense, and brutal. It was fought at such a close distance that as the Earps and Cowboys exchanged shots at one another, they could initially see into the whites of each other's eyes. Smoke created from the black powder from the firing revolvers filled the air and made it difficult for the combatants on either side to see what was happening, which is why many of the shots fired missed despite being at close range.

And while the movies often show McLaury Brothers and Billy Clanton each falling over and dying immediately after being hit, in reality, each took several minutes to die after being shot as they bled out. Tom in particular dragged himself several feet away from the fight before slowly expiring.

The gunfight at the OK Corral was anything but glamorous. The feelings of the survivors after the gunfight were perhaps best explained by Holliday. When the battle was over, he returned to his common-law wife, Kate, and sat down at the edge of the bed completely in shock over what had just happened.

"That was awful," Kate later claimed Holliday told her. "Just awful."

One would think that the O.K. Corral would have brought a halt to the feud between the Earps and the Cowboys with the Earps victorious. But as we'll explore in the next chapter, the gunfight did nothing to resolve the conflict and the feud would instead become even more violent in the coming months.

The Earps may have won at the O.K. Corral, but the Cowboys were about to take their revenge.

THE COWBOYS' REVENGE AGAINST THE EARPS

Many people are aware of the famous shootout at the O.K. Corral, but far fewer people are aware of the series of events that happened after. The Cowboys took revenge on the Earp brothers after the gunfight, murdering Morgan and severely wounding Virgil. This led to the Earp Vendetta Ride which would soon settle the conflict between the Earp and the Cowboys.

Things in Tombstone were about to get significantly worse after the gunfight at the OK Corral.

Once the gunfire ended and the smoke cleared, people from the surrounding homes and buildings began to emerge to inspect what had happened.

Three cowboys - Billy Clanton and Frank and Tom McLaury - were dead. Virgil and Morgan Earp and Doc Holliday were each wounded.

As Wyatt helped Virgil and Morgan get back to their homes, he was approached by Behan, who drew his revolver and told Wyatt he was under arrest.

After a few seconds, Wyatt retorted, "I won't be arrested today. I am right here and am not going away. You have deceived me. You told me these men were disarmed and I went to disarm them."

Behan then holstered his weapon and allowed Wyatt to move on with his brothers. They went to their homes where they were treated for their injuries by Doctor George Goodfellow.

A medical examination of the Cowboys after the gunfight found that Frank McLaury had been shot twice (once in the head and again in his abdomen), Tom McLaury had been shot with 12 buckshot rounds from Holliday's shotgun, and Billy Clanton had been shot three times (once in the wrist, once in the chest, and another in his abdomen).

The bodies of the three Cowboys were displayed in a window at the undertakers, where a sign was overlaid saying: "Murdered in the Streets of Tombstone."

In the coming days, nearly 2,500 people attended the funerals or watched from the sidewalks. Some people sided with the Earps and believed they had done the right thing, while others sided with the Cowboys and claimed that the Earps had deliberately provoked the fight.

****

Four days later, Ike Clanton filed murder charges against Earp and Holliday, which gave Behan the legal authority to arrest them. Wyatt and Holliday were arrested, while Virgil and Morgan were allowed to remain home to continue to recuperate but were still kept under tight watch.

The local Justice of the Peace, Wells Spicer, set Wyatt and Holliday's bail at $10,000, and this was paid by Wyatt's attorney and other local sympathetic business owners who pooled money together.

Spicer then convened a hearing to be held on October 31 to determine if there was enough evidence to set a trial.

For the next month, Spicer collected written and oral testimonies from many witnesses, which only created confusion as many of the accounts and testimonies were contradictory. For example, the witnesses were unable to agree on who had shot first in the gunfight.

Behan testified that the Cowboys did not initially resist and had thrown up their hands and that the gunfight was therefore instigated by the Earps and Holliday. Behan's testimony turned out to be very persuasive and changed the opinion of most of Tombstone's general public against the Earps and Holliday. Behan also testified that the McLaury brothers were not troublemakers and that Ike Clanton had been bullied by the Earps leading up to the gunfight.

Based on Behan's testimony, Spicer revoked Wyatt and Holliday's bail and had them jailed for the next two weeks.

However, continued testimony turned against the Cowboys in those coming weeks. The Cowboys' and Behan's entire testimony rested on the Cowboys throwing up their hands and the Earps and Holliday gunning them down anyway. Instead, further evidence showed that Billy Clanton and the McLaury brothers could not have received the gunshot wounds they received if their arms were in the air or in the positions where the testimonies had indicated. This completely contradicted Behan's testimony from earlier.

The Earp's defense team also showed that Virgil had acted within his legal limits as Tombstone's Marshal to attempt to disarm the Cowboys.

Based on this new evidence, Spicer ruled that there was not enough evidence to indict the Earps. However, he did make note of his belief that while Virgil was within his rights to deputize his brothers and Holliday before the shootout, it still may not have been the right thing to do.

****

The Earps had won at the O.K. Corral, and they had won in the courtroom in the aftermath of the gunfight. But that didn't turn much of the public opinion in their favor, and members of the Cowboy gang and those loyal to the gang began making continued death threats against them and Holliday. The Cowboys were thirsty for their revenge, and they made no secret of it.

Fearing for their safety, the Earps moved themselves and their families together to the Cosmopolitan Hotel, which was heavily guarded by other deputies and hired guns.

On the night of December 28, 1881, Virgil was on his way home to the Cosmopolitan from the Oriental Saloon. Suddenly, he was fired upon by three assailants hidden in the shadows and armed with double-barreled shotguns. The buckshot rounds shattered his entire upper left arm and several more rounds entered his back and lodged just above his groin.

The heavily wounded and bloodied Virgil managed to stagger into the hotel to his brothers, and doctors were immediately called.

The doctors considered amputating his left arm altogether, but instead, they were able to save it by removing several inches of the bone inside, including his elbow joint. Nonetheless, Virgil was crippled and would be unable to use his left arm for the rest of his life.

Virgil merely said to his wife, "At least I still have one arm left to hug you with."

Throughout the night it was unknown if Virgil would make it, and since his death was considered a big possibility due to his immense blood loss, the position of town marshal was passed to Wyatt. Nonetheless, Virgil managed to pull through and he spent several months recuperating in the Cosmopolitan.

Meanwhile, Wyatt decided to put together a posse to try to find Virgil's' assailants. Ike Clanton's hat had been found at the location where the three assailants were positioned, but the Cowboys created an alibi. Today, it is widely believed that Ike Clanton, Will McLaury (the brother of Tom and Frank), and Curly Bill Brocius were the shooters.

Following Virgil's shooting, anonymous letters and messages poured into Tombstone warning that anyone who sympathized or openly sided with the Earps would meet the same fate as Virgil.

The feud between the Earps and the Cowboys was no longer a feud at this point. Now it was a war.

****

Earp deputized Holliday, his younger brother Warren Earp, Jack "Turkey Creek" Johnson, John "Texas Jack" Vermillion, Sherman McMaster, Daniel "Tip" Tipton, and Charlie "Harlip" Smith to protect his family and pursue Virgil's assailants. Each of these men were experienced gunmen and some had even seen experience with the Texas Rangers or had worked with Wyatt before, so he knew he could trust them.

In January 1882, Wyatt obtained arrest warrants for the men he believed had ambushed Virgil. In the same month, Holliday and Johnny Ringo (one of the Cowboys and Curly Bill's right-hand man) exchanged violent threats that ended with both men being arrested.

Holliday was later released from jail, and he rode with Wyatt and his posse to Charleston, Arizona, where Ike Clanton was believed to be staying. Despite still being in jail, Ringo learned that the Earps were on their way to Charleston with the arrest warrants. He arranged for bail and Behan was able to release him before the bail payment came. Ringo then rode off to Charleston to warn Ike and the other Cowboys.

While enroute to Charleston, Wyatt and his posse were delayed when they came across Ben Maynard, a man who was known for associating with the Cowboys. The posse arrested Maynard, was joined by 30 other riders from Tombstone, and then proceeded to Charleston where they went door-to-door looking for Ike Clanton.

Ringo, as it turned out, had arrived in Charleston first and was able to warn Ike and the other Cowboys to get out of town before Wyatt and his posse arrived.

Ike believed that the arrest warrant was for armed robbery, and he surrendered with his brother Phin to Charley Bartholomew, a Wells Fargo agent. Ike believed that he would be let out again as he had in the past, but was instead surprised to learn that the warrant was for the attempted murder of Virgil.

At the trial, however, Ike got off clean again and the charges against him were dismissed. It was determined that there was not enough evidence to convict Ike in the shooting of Virgil. Even though his hat was found at the scene of the crime, many other people testified that Ike had been in Charleston at the time of the shooting.

Nonetheless, many people continued to believe that Ike had been one of the assailants who had fired a shot that maimed Virgil. This included Judge Stilwell, who told Wyatt after Ike's release, "You'll never clean up the crowd in this way. Next time, you'd better leave your prisoners in the brush where alibis don't count."

****

It didn't take long before the Cowboys struck again.

The Earps and Holliday continued to receive a never-ending stream of death threats from the Cowboys, but other than the ambush of Virgil, these threats were never acted upon…until March 18 of that year.

Morgan Earp, Doc Holliday, and their friend Dan Tipton attended a play production called *Stolen Kisses* at the local Schieffelin Hall, despite being warned that an attempt could be made on their lives. The two watched the play without incident, and afterward, an exhausted Holliday returned to his room to sleep.

Morgan went with Tipton to the Hatch Saloon and began playing pool. Wyatt was in the room as well with McMaster and Tipton and a few others.

Close to 11 o'clock that night, two shots were fired through the window of the backdoor: one at Wyatt and one at Morgan.

The bullet that was meant for Wyatt passed mere inches over his head and struck the wall, but the bullet meant for Morgan found its mark and struck him through the back, shattered his spine, and exited out his front.

Several men in the room rushed outside to find the assailant, but they found no one.

Morgan slumped over the pool table in a growing pool of blood. Wyatt called for doctors, and they tried in vain to remove the bullet. Goodfellow (who had treated Virgil and Morgan's gunshot wounds after the OK Corral) concluded that Morgan's wounds were fatal because of internal hemorrhaging.

Goodfellow advised Wyatt to allow Morgan to live the last few moments of his life in peace, and Morgan was transferred to a sofa in a nearby lounge. Before he passed away, Morgan whispered to Wyatt, "I can't see a damned thing."

Morgan and Wyatt had promised each other when they were younger that, in the event either of them was present when the other was dying, they would share what they could see before they died.

****

Several of the Cowboys had prepared for the Earp's inevitable retaliation by having Behan "arrest" them so they could be safely protected in Behan's jail. They were then released later, and no further arrests were made.

Wyatt Earp had had enough of the justice system and decided that the time had come to take matters into his own hands. One of his brothers had been killed and the other permanently maimed, and somehow, he had managed to miraculously escape a similar fate. Wyatt had not even been scratched at the O.K. Corral and the bullet meant for him at Morgan's assassination had missed him only fractionally.

The Cowboys were about to experience the full consequences of their failure to kill Wyatt Earp. To Wyatt, it was no longer just about enforcing the law and he was no longer interested in sending the Cowboys to jail. He decided that the only way to end the Cowboys once and for all and to protect his family was to set out and kill them all one by one.

The Cowboys may have taken revenge on the Earps, but now Wyatt was preparing to take his revenge against the Cowboys. None of them was prepared for what was coming.

THE EARP VENDETTA RIDE

Following the tragic events of the Cowboys' revenge, Wyatt and Holliday formed a posse to exact retaliation. This culminated in the Earp Vendetta Ride where Wyatt and Holliday took revenge on the Cowboys throughout Arizona Territory and settled the score with them once and for all.

On March 19, 1882, Wyatt, his brother James, and other members of Wyatt's posse were accompanying Virgil, Virgil's wife Allie, and the body of Morgan to the Benson train station.

It had been decided that James would transport Virgil, Allie, and Morgan's body back to the Earp's home in California, where Morgan would be buried by his parents and his wife.

Wyatt, however, received information that several of the Cowboys including Ike Clanton and Frank Stilwell would be waiting at the Tucson train station to ambush and murder Virgil.

Knowing that Virgil would have difficulty defending himself due to the loss of his left arm, Wyatt and his posse boarded the train so they could protect Virgil when the train arrived at Tucson. The posse included Wyatt's brother Morgan, Holliday, Turkey Creek Johnson, and Sherman McMaster.

Each man was armed with revolvers and rifles, while Wyatt was armed with a ten-gauge double-barreled shotgun.

When the train arrived in Tucson, they were to be greeted by Deputy US Marshal Joseph Evans. But as Virgil looked out the window from his train, he could see Clanton, Stilwell, and a few other cowboys lying in wait, in his words, "armed to the teeth" with rifles and shotguns themselves.

But when Clanton and Stilwell caught sight of Wyatt and the other members of his posse, along with Marshal Evans, they disappeared back into the crowd. Wyatt and his posse kept a sharp eye out as they escorted Virgil and Allie to Porter's Hotel where they all ate dinner before returning to the train later that night.

One of the other passengers, however, noticed Clanton, Stilwell, and other Cowboys positioning themselves behind the trains to ambush the group when they came back out.

At least one Cowboy was lying on top of one of the trains, while others were located behind the trains.

Wyatt, armed with his double-barreled shotgun, slipped between the trains to search for the men while the posse escorted Virgil and Allie back onto the train.

No one knows exactly what happened next, but between six and seven gunshots were heard and the following morning, Stillwell's body was discovered mangled by two buckshot wounds and three pistol and rifle gunshot wounds.

One witness described Stilwell as the "worst shot-up man" he had ever seen. Ike Clanton, however, got away.

****

After verifying that the train was safely on its way to the Earp home in California, Wyatt and his posse returned to Benson to pick up their horses. The posse only had one mission: to hunt down and kill as many of the Cowboys as they could. Frank Stillwell had just been the beginning.

But now Wyatt Earp was a wanted man. News of Stillwell's death at the Tucson train station had spread quickly, and Pima County Sheriff Bob Paul sent a telegram to Behan asking him to arrest Wyatt. Wyatt Earp was now both a lawman and a wanted man at the same time.

Wyatt was lucky though. The office manager at the telegraph office happened to be a personal friend of his, and he showed the message to Wyatt before Behan. Wyatt and his posse then saddled their horses and were preparing to leave when they were confronted by Behan and five deputies.

The two sides stared each other down, and for a brief moment, it appeared possible that the O.K. Corral shootout would erupt all over again.

"Wyatt, I want to see you," Behan ordered with his hand over his revolver.

"You might see me once too often," Wyatt retorted.

The Earp posse then mounted their horses before riding out of town, and Behan and his deputies made no effort to prevent them from leaving. The incident was widely interpreted as a weakhanded effort by Behan to arrest Wyatt.

Outside of Tombstone, Wyatt's posse met up with Texas Jack Vermillion, Dan Tipton, Fred Dodge, Charlie Smith, Louis Cooley, and Johnny Green to expand the strength of the posse. They rode around the territory in search of members of the Cowboy gang to kill.

Behan, meanwhile, formed his own posse that consisted of several Cowboys, including Johnny Ringo, Ike Clanton, Ike's brother Phineas, and nearly 20 other men. They mounted their horses and rode out of Tombstone to search for Wyatt's posse.

The Earp posse and the Cowboys posse were at war with one another, and both claimed to have the law on their side.

****

The Earp's posse began to hunt down and eliminate several members of the Cowboy gang while evading Behan's posse. Wyatt led his men up into the mountains in search of Florentino "Indian Charlie" Cruz, a known associate of the Cowboys. Cruz's body was found a day later with no less than ten gunshot wounds. Wyatt later claimed that before they killed him, Cruz had admitted to taking part in Morgan's murder and identified Johnny Ringo, Ike Clanton, and Curly Bill Brocius as the others who had taken part in the assassination.

Following the killing of Cruz, Smith and Tipton returned to Tombstone for money and to find information. After they arrived in town, however, they were discovered by Behan who promptly arrested them. Both men paid their bond, and Smith returned to the posse while Tipton remained in town. Wyatt instructed Tipton to return to Tombstone to raise money to cover the posse's expenses and told him to rejoin the posse at Iron Springs.

Wyatt and the posse then traveled to Iron Springs in the Whetstone Mountains, although the definitive location is unknown to this day.

Somehow, however, the Cowboy posse had gained word that the Earp posse would be traveling to the springs and were lying in wait. With the posse riding toward the spring, Wyatt elected to ride ahead of the group, and he also loosened the two gun belts he wore around his hip for comfort.

What happened next was incredible and remarkable, and proved yet again about how lucky Wyatt was.

Wyatt ended up riding almost directly into the Cowboy camp! He was in the process of dismounting his horse, when the Cowboys gang, who were all hidden behind trees and rocks, carefully took aim at Wyatt and opened fire.

Despite over a dozen men firing upon him at once from all directions, not a single bullet struck Wyatt and instead hit the ground or whizzed right past him. When the shooting started, Wyatt's gun belts that he had loosened dropped down his legs. He had to bend down to bring the belts back up to his hip - while still under fire from all directions - before he could draw his revolvers and return fire.

The rest of the Earp gang behind Wyatt heard the gunfire and immediately sped up. Texas Jack arrived first, but his horse was shot and killed from under him. Nonetheless, Texas Jack was able to regain his feet and remain close to Wyatt as he fired back at the Cowboys.

Holliday, Johnson, and McMaster arrived next and took cover while returning fire.

Curly Bill aimed his shotgun at Wyatt and fired but missed. Spotting Curly Bill and with his revolvers out of ammunition, Wyatt tossed them aside and calmly withdrew his double-barreled shotgun from the scabbard on his saddle. He then took careful aim at Curly Bill and fired two rounds of buckshot, both of which struck Curly Bill and nearly ripped him apart in two.

Killed instantly, Curly Bill fell back into the water at the end of the springs, to the utter shock and disbelief of the other Cowboys.

The Earp posse continued to fire back against the Cowboys before remounting their horses and falling back. None of the Earp's posse was killed in the shootout, but McMaster had been grazed. Besides Curly Bill, one other Cowboy had been shot in the chest and killed and another had been shot in the arm and wounded.

Yet again, Wyatt Earp was extraordinarily lucky. When the shootout was over, his jacket and hat were riddled with bullet holes, the spurs on his boots had been shot off, and his saddle horn on his horse had been shot off as well - but not a single bullet had come into contact with his body.

Wyatt had survived without a scratch at the O.K. Corral, and he had missed the bullet that was meant for him at Morgan's assassination, but the gunbattle at Iron Springs was perhaps the most extraordinary fight that he had ever come out of unscathed.

News of Curly Bill's death and Wyatt miraculously escaping getting shot again at Iron Springs spread around in the newspapers and reinforced Wyatt's image as an invincible lawman.

****

Behan formed a new posse to hunt down the Earp crew in response to what happened at Iron Springs. The new posse consisted of no less than 25 men and included Johnny Ringo and Ike and Phineas Clanton.

Behan also again arrested Smith, whom Wyatt had sent back to Tombstone to collect money for the posse.

In desperate need of money and a place to hide out, the Earp posse traveled to the ranch of Henry Hooker, who congratulated Earp for taking down Curly Bill. He provided the posse with a place to eat and sleep.

One of Hooker's men spotted Behan's posse nearby and alerted Hooker, who then recommended to Wyatt that he make a defensive stand there. Not wanting to endanger Hooker or his family, Wyatt instead moved his men to a series of hills about three miles away.

Behan and his posse then arrived on the ranch, only to be met with disgust by Hooker, who denied giving Behan any help or information. Behan's posse would never catch up with Earp.

Earp's posse began to go their separate ways after three weeks of riding together. They knew that they would not receive a fair trial for the killing of Frank Stillwell weeks before and would need to return to areas of the United States with an established Federal and state judicial system for their own protection. Wyatt and Holliday traveled north to Colorado, while the other members of the posse went their own ways across the country.

Even though the "Earp Vendetta Ride," as it came to be known, was officially over, several members of the Cowboy gang (including Johnny Ringo, Billy Claiborne, and Ike Clanton) were killed over the coming years, including some under mysterious circumstances.

Ringo in particular was discovered dead by a tree with a bullet hole in his head. He and Holliday had long held a grudge against one another, so legend has it that Holliday returned to settle the score with Ringo. Hollywood movies popularize this version of events, but to this day, no one knows for sure who killed Ringo or if he took his own life instead.

****

Holliday died only a few years after the Vendetta Ride at a Sanitorium in Colorado. Wyatt visited him one last time shortly before his death.

Wyatt Earp would continue to embark on adventures for the next 50 years. When the Vendetta Ride was over, he traveled to San Francisco to reconnect with his common-law wife Josephine (he had sent her away from Tombstone when the conflict with the Cowboys had gotten worse).

Wyatt and Josephine would travel the West together for the rest of their lives.

Earp became a lawman in Kootenai County, Idaho, when gold was discovered there, before returning to California with Josephine. At the turn of the century, he and Josephine traveled to Alaska to join the Gold Rush there, before returning to Seattle and then California again. Along the way, Wyatt refereed boxing matches, invested in real estate, opened up several saloons and gambling halls, and acquired a small fortune.

He did, however, attract controversy for allegedly fixing boxing matches and card games at the saloons he ran as a source of profit, and these controversies overshadowed his actions at Tombstone throughout the latter part of his life. Many people who knew Wyatt at the time remarked that these controversies and the negative publicity they had generated deeply bothered him.

It was because of these controversies that Wyatt sought to rehabilitate his image, and he worked with several writers to put his biography on the page so the general public could hear his version of events. The most famous book about Wyatt was written by Stuart Lake, who conducted eight interviews with him during the research and writing process. It was written as a biography in the first person.

While many people regard the events in this biography as being deliberately exaggerated in favor of Wyatt and the Earp brothers, the book succeeded in making sure Wyatt's exploits and reputation as a lawman in Dodge City and Tombstone became more well-known to the public than the controversies of his later life.

These stories effectively cemented Wyatt's reputation as the stoic, tough, and fearless Western Frontier Marshal that most people know him as today. This image was further reinforced in countless movies and TV shows that were made about his life that became popular with the public, including *My Darling Clementine*, *Gunfight at the O.K Corral*, *Hour of the Gun*, *Tombstone*, and *Wyatt Earp*.

Toward the end of his life, Wyatt lived in Los Angeles and actually consulted with many film directors, producers, and actors who were making Western movies to help ensure realism in these productions. Among the famous names Wyatt was known to have personally worked with included John Ford, Charlie Chaplin, Raoul Walsh, and John Wayne, and all of them stated later that they were impressed by Wyatt.

Wyatt Earp passed away in 1929 at the age of 80, but he is well-remembered today as the most famous lawman of the Old West era.

A quote from an interview with Wyatt Earp:

For my handling of the situation at Tombstone, I have no regrets. Were it to be done over again, I would do exactly as I did at that time. If the outlaws and their friends and allies imagined that they could intimidate or exterminate the Earps by a process of murder, and then hide behind alibis and the technicalities of the law, they simply missed their guess. I want to call your particular attention again to one fact, which writers of Tombstone incidents and history apparently have overlooked: with the deaths of the McLaurys, the Clantons, Stillwell, Florentino Cruz, Curly Bill, and the rest, organized, politically protected crime and depredations in Cochise County ceased.

THE ASSASSINATION
OF JESSE JAMES

Jesse James was one of the most famous robbers of the Old West. Fancying himself as a modern-day Robin Hood, James found himself beloved by much of the general public. James likely never expected that his end would come via assassination by a member of his own gang.

Wyatt Earp is a famous name that even those who are not familiar with Western history have heard of.

Jesse James is another equally famous name.

But whereas Wyatt Earp was famous as a tough-as-nails lawman, Jesse James was famous as a capture-evading outlaw.

During his short life, Jesse and his gang robbed stagecoaches, trains, and banks all over the Midwest with his gang and attained celebrity status and both notoriety and admiration. Some viewed Jesse as a detestable outlaw who deserved to be hanged, while others viewed him as the Robin Hood of the West.

One young man, Robert Ford, was one of Jesse's admirers. Having followed Jesse's criminal career, he decided he wanted to not only meet him but join his gang.

The fates of these two men were about to collide.

****

Jesse James was born in 1847 in Missouri. He had one older brother, Frank, and a younger sister, Susan.

Jesse's father, Robert, was a minister. When Jesse was just three years old, his father died while preaching to those taking part in the California gold rush. Jesse's mother, Zerelda, remarried a man named Benjamin Simms in 1852. Simms was very cruel to Jesse and his brother Frank, but he passed away two years later. Zerelda then became remarried again to Dr. Reuben Samuel, with whom she had four more children.

The James-Samuel household lived on a tobacco farm, and they owned seven slaves.

When the Civil War broke out in 1861, Missouri was in a unique position. Not only was it a border state, but its population was also divided between the Union and the Confederacy. Violence had erupted between pro-slavery and anti-slavery militias in the years leading up to the outbreak of the war.

But whereas conventional armies confronted each other on the battlefields of Virginia to the East, Missouri was witness primarily to guerilla warfare by both sides. The Confederate guerilla forces were known as the "bushwhackers," while Union guerilla forces were called "jayhawkers."

Both sides committed vast atrocities during the war; raids on innocent families in homes and executions without trial were regular occurrences.

The James-Samuel family was on the Confederate side during the war. In 1861, Frank James left to go fight in the war, but he returned home when he became sick, and later joined a bushwhacker guerilla group. A jayhawker group came to the James-Samuel farm on the hunt for the guerilla group that Frank was in. They hung Reuben from a tree (and then cut him down before he could die) and whipped 16-year-old Jesse before departing from the farm.

The incident left a profound effect on Jesse, and he decided to join the same guerilla group as Frank. The two brothers gained much combat experience during their service in the war, but both brothers also took part in horrific atrocities as well, including the Lawrence and Centralia massacres that saw hundreds of Union soldiers and civilians mercilessly slaughtered by the bushwhacker Confederates.

In the summer of 1864, Jesse was shot in the chest during battle, but he survived by retreating to his uncle's boarding house where he was tended to by his cousin, Zerelda "Zee" Mimms. Jesse and Zee began a courtship as he made his recovery, which would eventually lead to their marriage in 1874.

****

When the Civil War ended with the defeat of the Confederacy in 1865, Missouri was more bitterly divided than ever. The Civil War may have concluded, but the violence in Missouri did not as veterans from pro-Union and pro-Confederate gangs continued to clash. The pro-Reconstruction state legislature of Missouri passed several anti-Confederate laws, including laws that freed slaves and denied former Confederates from holding office.

In this highly volatile and violent environment, several Confederate bushwhacker veterans, including some who had been associates of Frank and Jesse during the war, began to launch attacks and robberies against pro-Reconstruction officials and former jayhawker officers.

The first robbery that Jesse and Frank James are believed to have participated in was the Clay County Savings Association Robbery, in which pro-Confederate forces robbed a bank owned by former Union militia officers.

Jesse and Frank then proceeded to commit several more robberies across Missouri, most of which were directed against these former Union or pro-Reconstruction officials. Their robberies targeted local banks with smaller capital rather than larger banks because they claimed they were only attempting to harm locals and officials who were pro-Union.

The James brothers' fame began to spread across the state, and their actions either received praise or scorn from people depending on whether they were sympathetic to the Confederate cause or pro-Reconstruction.

In 1869, Jesse and most likely Frank robbed the Daviess County Savings Association. Jesse gunned down an innocent man (John Sheets) because he believed him to be Samuel Cox, the man who had killed one of his commanders,

William "Bloody Bill" Anderson, during the war. After the shooting and robbery, Jesse and Frank managed to evade a large posse that was sent after them, further adding to their notoriety.

By this time, Jesse and Frank had been branded as outlaws, and Thomas Crittenden, the Governor of Missouri, had put out a reward for their capture. Jesse and Frank knew that public support was now turning against them, so they formed an alliance with John Newman Edwards, who was the founder and editor of the *Kansas City Times*.

Edwards, who himself was still sympathetic to the Confederate cause, received multiple letters from Jesse that he published in his newspapers. In these letters, Jesse defended his actions by claiming that he was only continuing the fight against the pro-Union and pro-Reconstruction forces. He said he had no intention of harming anyone who was pro-Confederate.

As a result of these letters, which gained widespread publicity as well, Jesse's fame across the country increased significantly. Many people viewed him as a Robin Hood-type hero who was still fighting the good fight for the Confederate cause. However, many others viewed him as a violent criminal and a public menace who needed to be eliminated once and for all.

Southern Democrats and those who were still loyal to the idea of the Confederacy loved Jesse James, while Northern Republicans and those loyal to the Union and Reconstruction of the South hated him.

****

Just like Billy the Kid, who we discussed in an earlier chapter, Frank and Jesse James had an unusual knack for being able to quickly commit their crimes and robberies before successfully evading the lawmen and posses sent out to capture or kill them.

The brothers' robberies continued into the 1870s, during which they joined forces with the Younger Gang consisting of brothers John, Jim, and Bob, each of whom were also former Confederates. Jesse, however, would remain the most famous member of the gang.

The James-Younger Gang, as it came to be known, robbed banks and stagecoaches all over the United States, with robberies taking place in Missouri, Iowa, West Virginia, and Texas. Throughout this time, Edwards continued to publish

James's letters and perpetuate the image of Jesse James as a modern-day Robin Hood.

By 1874, the Pinkerton National Detective Agency was on the hunt for Jesse James. The Pinkertons were known professionals who worked to stop criminals, but they met their match with the James-Younger gang. Every Pinkerton agent sent after Jesse James and his gang was killed.

By 1874, Allan Pinkerton, the founder of the Pinkertons, had had enough and decided to take on the James-Younger gang himself. He met up with former Unionists who lived near Jesse's childhood farm and launched a late-night attack against the property.

The Pinkerton men came to the property silently and then threw explosives into the house that killed James' younger half-brother and blew off the arm of his mother, Zerelda.

The attack on the farm gained national attention and only caused more people to sympathize with Jesse. In fact, the Missouri Legislature was only narrowly able to defeat a bill that would have granted a full amnesty and pardon to Jesse!

Pinkerton continued to pursue the James gang but always came up short. Finally, when the railroad withdrew their financial support of Pinkerton and more of his men were killed by the gang, he gave up the chase.

****

Jesse James may have evaded the Pinkertons, which was something that few other outlaws achieved, but his luck didn't last for long after that.

In 1876, the James-Younger gang launched an ill-fated robbery attempt on the First National Bank in Minnesota that would prove to be their undoing.

The James-Younger gang arrived in Minnesota with the First National Bank targeted because its investors were former Union officials. It was meant to be just another robbery against their old enemies, but things went wrong almost as soon as the robbery began.

The cashier who happened to be in the bank at the time, Joseph Lee Heywood, was a stalwart man who refused to open the safe even after being pistol-whipped over the head and having a knife blade pressed against his throat. In a fit of rage, one member of the gang raised his revolver and shot Heywood directly in the head, ending their chances of withdrawing any money from the safe since Heywood was the only one in the bank who could open it.

The robbery was already a bust, and to make matters worse for the outlaws, citizens witnessing the robbery outside alerted the local law enforcement officials, who then surrounded the bank.

The James-Younger game was forced to shoot their way out of town, and while they managed to escape, two members of the gang were gunned down and several more were wounded. The local law enforcement formed a large posse to track down the gang.

Frank and Jesse split from the three Younger brothers and fled south to Missouri. Meanwhile, the posse caught up with the Youngers and forced each of them to surrender.

That was the end of the James-Younger gang.

****

The robberies and exploits of Jesse James and his gang were gaining nationwide attention, but one young man, in particular, was following the news of the gang very closely: Robert Ford.

Ford had been reading the letters that Edwards had been publishing and came to idolize Jesse James. He dreamed of meeting him and joining his gang.

After the disaster at the attempted First National Bank Robbery, Jesse and Frank elected to lay low in Missouri. They assumed new identities and lived a quiet life for three years, but the excitement of robbing banks proved to be too much of a temptation for Jesse to overcome. Against the wishes of Frank, who wanted to continue living lawfully, Jesse put a new gang together to resume robberies in 1879.

One of the men who joined James' new gang was Ford.

The first robbery of Jesse's new gang took place in late 1879 when they held up a train just outside of Glendale, Missouri. They then proceeded to undertake several new robberies across Mississippi and Alabama.

James's new gang, however, did not garner the same level of success as his older gang from the James-Younger days. The members of the new gang were not seasoned veterans or as disciplined as Jesse's old gang. Their lack of experience showed as several members were killed by the lawmen sent to pursue them, with Jesse and Frank only narrowly escaping with their lives on multiple occasions.

Furthermore, there was turmoil within the gang, and Jesse himself murdered one of his own gang members because he did not trust him. Most of the other members of the gang were eventually either captured or killed.

Soon, there were only four members of the gang left: Jesse, Frank, Robert Ford and his brother Charley.

By 1881, Jesse had returned to nearby his family home in Missouri with Frank. The two brothers decided that the time had come to give up their life of crime and live a quiet life after all. But the window of opportunity for that was gone.

If Jesse had agreed with Frank to live quietly in 1876, chances are high that he would have gotten away and been allowed to live the rest of his life in peace. Trying to start a new gang to resume his robberies in 1879 would turn out to be the biggest mistake that Jesse ever made.

Jesse's days were numbered, and little did he know that the danger wasn't from somebody outside the gang - rather, it was somebody within.

Jesse allowed Charley and Robert to move into his family house. They were the only two men besides Frank whom he trusted at that point, and he also believed that the two brothers could help him out in any potential gunfight that came their way.

Ford, though, had other plans and took advantage of Jesse's trust. Even though he had idolized Jesse in the years prior, Ford had grown tired of him since and the idea of the massive $5,000 reward that was on his head had become more appealing to him. Ford also wanted to be known as "the man who had shot Jesse James" because of the national fame and attention that this was sure to have given him.

Ford went to Governor Crittenden and revealed that he was a part of the James gang. What Ford and Crittenden discussed exactly remains a mystery to this day, but it is widely speculated that Ford discussed either capturing or killing Jesse and bringing him in either dead or alive in exchange for the reward money and that Crittenden agreed.

This meeting attracted significant controversy because if Crittenden agreed to the killing of Jesse by Ford, it would have meant he was consenting to the killing of a private citizen by another private citizen.

Regardless of what Ford and Crittenden discussed exactly, Ford left the meeting and returned to Jesse's home later that day.

On April 3, 1882, Robert Ford made his move.

****

Jesse James took off his gun belt, which included his two holstered revolvers, and set it down on the sofa before climbing up on a chair to clean a dusty picture on the wall.

Ford walked up behind the unarmed Jesse. He then drew his revolver, cocked the hammer, and shot Jesse right in the back of the head.

Jesse was killed instantly, and he fell hard to the floor by Ford's feet.

Immediately following the assassination, Ford wired Crittenden that he had killed Jesse James. Excited to claim the reward money, Ford and his brother Charley then turned themselves in to the authorities. To their surprise and dismay, they were instead charged with first-degree murder and arrested.

However, Crittenden quickly pardoned both of the brothers, but he only paid $500 instead of the promised $5,000 reward money. He gave the rest of the reward money to the local sheriff. Likely Crittenden did this to hide the fact that he knew Ford was going to assassinate Jesse from their meeting beforehand.

The Ford brothers then traveled out of Missouri to escape the wrath of those who were on Jesse's side.

Meanwhile, the assassination of Jesse James sent shockwaves across America. Those who hated him were elated to hear the news, while those who loved him were overwhelmed with sorrow and went into mourning.

Ford was already upset that he didn't get all of the promised reward money, but things were about to get worse for him. Ford had expected to gain fame and praise for being the man who killed Jesse James. He attempted to profit off of the assassination by traveling the country and hosting reenactments of the shooting.

Instead, Ford was widely labeled as a coward. Those who supported Jesse condemned Ford for his actions and called him a murderer, while those who were against Jesse believed that Ford should have captured Jesse at gunpoint so he could have been brought to trial instead.

In 1892, a Jesse James sympathizer named Edward O'Kelley walked into a saloon that Ford was operating with a double-barreled shotgun. He walked right up to Ford, said,

"Hello Bob," and then shot Ford at point-blank range with both barrels. Ford was killed instantly.

Kelley was pardoned ten years into the life-in-prison sentence he received due to thousands of signatures petitioning for his release.

Public opinion of Jesse James remains heavily divided to this day, but there's no denying that he went down as one of the most famous outlaws of the Old West, if not the most famous.

Was Jesse James a hero or an outlaw, and if the latter, should Ford have shot him down the way he did or brought him in for a trial instead? Only you can decide the answers to those questions for yourself.

GERONIMO'S REVENGE

When his family was brutally murdered by Mexican soldiers armed with rifles, the famous Apache warrior Geronimo exacted revenge using only a knife. His continued desire for revenge fueled his several decades-long struggles against Mexican and American soldiers.

The name "one who yawns" doesn't exactly conjure up images in the mind of a furious and passionate warrior who strikes fear in his enemies.

But that's exactly who Geronimo was.

Geronimo is perhaps the most famous name that came out of the United States-Apache wars, which were fought throughout the latter half of the 1800s in the American Southwest. Originally a medicine man from the Chiricahua Apache tribe, Geronimo gained prominence for his valiant battle against Mexican and U.S. military forces in Mexico, Arizona, and New Mexico.

The Apache tribe violently resisted being moved onto reservations when the United States began pushing west. This was because the Apache were a nomadic people who didn't like the idea of being moved to a single place, and they weren't afraid to turn to battle to stop this from happening.

Before the United States arrived and began moving Native Americans to reservations, the Apache had already been fighting against the Spanish and Mexican peoples for literally hundreds of years. These centuries of combat experience helped them in their fight against the Americans, as the U.S. Army found the Apache to be among the fiercest groups of Native Americans they would ever fight.

Geronimo was perhaps the fiercest of them all.

****

Contrary to what many people think, the Apache are not one tribe of people but many. The term "Apache" actually refers to a *group* of Native American tribes that are culturally related. Examples of specific Apache tribes include the Kiowa, Lipan, Mescalero, Chiricahua, and Jicarilla.

These tribes were mainly located in what is now Arizona, New Mexico, Colorado, Texas, Oklahoma, and Mexico.

The Apache had begun fighting the Spanish in the 1600s, with the two sides launching raids against one another. When Mexico was founded in the 1820s, the fighting with the Apache didn't cease but rather became amplified. In the 1820s, thousands of Mexican soldiers and civilians alike were killed by Apache warriors, and over a hundred settlements were raided and destroyed.

Apache attacks against Mexican settlers were so substantial that the Mexican military was forced to establish multiple forts in the sole part of the country and place bounties on Apache scalps. Mexican soldiers would embark on expeditions from these forts to track down and kill Apache warriors, before returning to rest and resupply. The forts then hindered attacks from Apache forces.

Unable to attack the well-fortified Mexican forts, the Apache instead targeted Mexican settlements and villages. Raiding communities such as these became a part of the Apache way of life, not only for combat purposes against their opponents but for economic benefit as well. The Apache would plunder horses, livestock, guns, weapons, food, and other valuables.

The Mexican retaliations against the Apache were, however, no less bloody, and many Apache encampments were raided and burned to the ground as well.

One of the Apache warriors leading the Apache struggle against the Mexicans was Geronimo.

****

Geronimo was born in what is now New Mexico in 1829 as part of the Chiricahua tribe. When he was 22, Geronimo traveled south into Old Mexico to trade, along with other members of his tribe. They traded there for several days.

The Mexicans and Apache had been at war with each other for years at this point, however, truces were sometimes called. In his later life, Geronimo would recall how even though the Apache and Mexicans hated one another, these truces were meant to be respected and typically were.

There was a truce in place during Geronimo's trading journey to Old Mexico. However, while there, Geronimo learned from visiting Apache women that the truce had been broken.

It was then that Geronimo discovered the most horrific truth that would wound his heart for the rest of his life.

While he had been away trading, 400 Mexican troops had attacked his camp back home. All the horses were taken, all the warriors were killed, and many of the women and children were massacred as well. The attack was conducted in retaliation for an Apache raid that had occurred a few days prior.

The attack was brutal. According to the visiting tribeswomen, among the dead were Geronimo's mother, his wife, whom he had married five years earlier, and his three children.

Geronimo raced back to the site of the camp. When he arrived, he had to sneak into the camp to try to identify the bodies since the Mexican soldiers were still present.

But the terrible news was confirmed when he found the slain corpses of his mother, wife, and children. Geronimo turned around and walked to the river, where he stood for countless hours trying to process what had happened.

This event served as the most significant turning point in Geronimo's life. He cast aside his identity as a medicine man and vowed to take up arms to fight back against his enemies.

That night, Geronimo joined a war council. The council decided that since they were too few in numbers to fight successfully back against the Mexicans, they would travel north and return to their homelands in Arizona.

"I stood until all had passed, hardly knowing what I would do," Geronimo would later say. "I had no weapon, nor did I hardly wish to fight, nor did I contemplate recovering the bodies of my loved ones, for that was forbidden. I did not pray, nor did I resolve to do anything in particular, for I had no purpose left. I finally followed the tribe silently, keeping just within hearing distance of the soft noise of the feet of the retreating Apache."

Geronimo's emotions swelled further when he returned home and saw the toys and decorations that his wife and children had made. He burned the family's teepee and destroyed all of their property.

But even in this overwhelming moment of grief, Geronimo was able to find a new purpose in life. He vowed revenge that day against the Mexican soldiers who had taken his family, and he allowed his happy memories of his family in the months and years prior and the knowledge that he could never relive those memories ever again, to fuel his desire for revenge.

****

Knowing that he couldn't take on the Mexican army on his own, Geronimo convened Apache from several different tribes together.

"Kinsmen," Geronimo later recalled saying to the Apache warriors who had gathered at one of his councils. "You have heard what the Mexicans have recently done without cause. You are my relatives - uncles, cousins, brothers. We are men the same as the Mexicans are - we can do to them what they have done to us. Let us go forward and trail them. I will lead you to their city. We will attack them in their homes. I will fight in the front of the battle. I only ask you to follow me to avenge this wrong done by these Mexicans. Will you come?"

Many of the warriors were very wary of the idea of joining Geronimo, a medicine man, to fight. Geronimo had never fought in battle before, but the powerful emotion that showed in his voice and the persuasiveness of his words helped convince several warriors to join his cause and fight back against the Mexicans.

Geronimo set several rules for the warriors who would fight with him. The first was that no one was to mourn himself or any other Apache warrior who fought with him if they were slain.

The second was that no relatives of any warrior killed could blame any other Apache warrior who fought with them. This was because each of the warriors had agreed to go fight knowing full well what the risks were.

The third was that each warrior would need to travel light, with each man carrying three days' rations and using a single piece of cloth as both clothing and a blanket at night.

The fourth was that the warriors would hunt and kill game along the way to resupply themselves as they moved.

"Our arrows were all gone, our spears broken off in the bodies of our dead enemies," Geronimo said when recounting how lightly armed his band of warriors was: "We only had our hand knives with which to fight."

To keep their movements concealed, Geronimo's war party traveled high in the mountains and by rivers to avoid detection by the Mexican settlers in the lower parts of the terrain.

Geronimo had no interest in attacking these Mexican settlements and plundering them along the way as the Apache had often done before. He had only one mission: to find and kill the same Mexican soldiers who had massacred his family.

****

Geronimo's war party arrived at Arispe, a military fort where he believed the Mexican soldiers who had killed his family were stationed.

Eight Mexican soldiers rode out to parley with the Apache, but Geronimo's war party killed and scalped all eight of them, before sending the scalps back to the fort in an attempt to lure the rest of the Mexican forces out.

Sure enough, the plan worked. The following day, more Mexican soldiers ventured out of the fort to engage with the Apache, but they were all killed too, and Geronimo's warriors took their guns.

The following day after that, the Mexicans sent out even more men to engage the Apache. Geronimo would recall later in life how no less than four Mexican companies, two of infantry and two of cavalry, came out of the fort in an attempt to fight him in a conventional battle.

Observing the soldiers from afar, Geronimo recognized several of their faces as exactly the same ones that he had seen at the encampment where his family had been murdered.

Geronimo pulled his warriors back toward the river. The Mexican infantry appeared over the hill with the cavalry in the rear. When the Mexican infantry advanced to within 400 yards of the Mexican position, they opened fire with their muskets.

The Apache allowed the initial volley to pass over, and then while the Mexicans were reloading their rifles, Geronimo sprung his attack.

The battle was ferocious, bloody, and close quarter. Each side was merciless as many men on both sides were shot, scalped, stabbed, sliced, and bludgeoned.

Geronimo recalled: "In all the battle I thought of my murdered mother, wife, and babies - of my father's grave and my vow of vengeance, and I fought with fury. Many fell by my hand, and constantly I led the advance. Many braves were killed."

The battle would last for two hours, and when it was over, all of the Mexicans appeared to be killed.

While Geronimo and the other Apache were resting, two Mexican soldiers who had appeared to be dead suddenly sprang up. They shot down two of the Apache warriors next to Geronimo and then charged forward with their sabers drawn.

Geronimo and another Apache engaged them with spears. The other Apache was soon struck down, making Geronimo the only one left. He stabbed one of the two Mexican soldiers with his spear, and then he tackled the other Mexican soldier with his bare hands. During the struggle, Geronimo drew his knife and stabbed the soldier multiple times until he bled out and died.

Geronimo then picked up the dead soldier's spear and went around the battlefield prodding the bodies with the blade to make sure they were all dead. Around him, the surviving Apache warriors cried out in victory.

"Over the bloody field, covered with the bodies of Mexicans, rang the fierce Apache war-whoop," he recalled. "Still covered with the blood of my enemies, still holding my conquering weapon, still hot with the joy of battle, victory, and vengeance, I was surrounded by the Apache braves and made war chief of all the Apache."

****

Geronimo's struggle against the Mexicans, and later the Americans, didn't end that day. It just started. He would continue to bear ill will toward Mexican soldiers for the rest of his life because he could never forgive what had happened to his family. Many accounts of Geronimo's life state that while he was a very cunning and courageous warrior, the brutality he demonstrated was always more extreme for Mexican soldiers than it was for American soldiers, even though Geronimo fought hard against both groups.

Geronimo turned his attention to fighting the Americans when they invaded Apache lands during the American-Mexican War in 1848. During this war, America gained control of the land that would one day become California, Arizona, New Mexico, and Texas.

Throughout the next several decades, Geronimo would fight guerilla campaigns against the American soldiers sent out to capture or kill him. Each time Geronimo was captured and held in a reservation, he and other warriors being held in captivity would fight their way out and resume the struggle.

It wasn't until the mid-1880s that an aged Geronimo came to accept that the Apache would have to live with the reservations, and he surrendered for the final time to an American military detachment sent to capture him.

Geronimo died as a prisoner of war in 1909, at the age of 79. He was buried at Fort Sill in the Beef Creek Apache Cemetery.

CAMELS OF
THE OLD WEST

Aren't camels supposed to be from Arabia and the Sahara? That's where they come from, but little do most people know that camels were brought to work in the American Southwest as well. This chapter covers the reasons why camels were brought to the American West, how they were used, and why they didn't end up becoming a bigger presence despite their usefulness.

In 1883, there was a mysterious creature that was said to haunt Arizona Territory.

Known as the Red Ghost, the creature was said to be massive, stand on four legs, have a reddish fur coat, and be unlike anything else that lived in the area.

It was also said to be incredibly dangerous, having trampled a woman to death when she unwisely approached the creature.

One cowboy had attempted to catch the elusive and dangerous creature, only for the animal to demonstrate immense strength when it broke free of his rope and then charged his horse, nearly killing him.

Throughout the rest of the year, a few homesteaders, miners, and cattlemen were only able to observe a few quick glimpses of the creature before it disappeared back into the heatwaves of the Arizona desert.

A group of miners were working along a river one day when they suddenly saw the Red Ghost walking along the water. They drew their guns and fired at the animal only for it to take off running and disappear into the heatwaves again.

But something fell from the animal's back when it took off running, and when the miners inspected it, it was none other than a human skull with skin, dried blood, and hair still attached to it.

Then one day after that incident, a rancher spotted the Red Ghost grazing nonchalantly in his tomato patch. Intrigued, the rancher ran back inside to grab his rifle. Stepping back out, he aimed at the creature and fired.

The Red Ghost was struck by the bullet, staggered, and then fell over dead right in the middle of the patch.

Elated, the rancher ran up to the creature to see what he had shot.

The Red Ghost, it turned out, was…a camel!

****

The camel the rancher had shot had leather strappings wrapped around its back. When the story reached the local newspapers, it was suggested that a person had been lashed to the back of the camel and died, but the beast continued to carry the lashed body anyway. The presence of the dead body on the back of the camel was why the camel looked so unrecognizable in its many brief sightings.

The Red Ghost was not the only camel sighting in the Old West during that time. Many more sightings of camels continued for decades after that up to the 1920s.

But why?

Camels are indigenous to Northern Africa, the Middle East, and Asia. How did camels make it across the Atlantic to North America?

Let's find out.

Horses and mules were by far the most widely used pack animals in the Old West and had been for decades. But in

141

1836, Major George Crosman encouraged the U.S. War Department to transfer camels over to the United States from the Middle East.

The War Department conducted a study on the usefulness of camels as pack animals and concluded that Crosman was correct that camels could be useful. This sentiment was also shared by Senator Jefferson Davis, who later became famous as the President of the Confederacy.

Even though horses, mules, and oxen had proven to be more than adequate pack animals, it was believed that camels would have the unique advantage of being able to operate with little water in hot and arid regions, particularly in the Southwest.

In 1855, the United States Congress elected to spend $30,000 (equal to almost a million dollars in today's money) to import camels into the United States to serve with the military on expeditions that involved traveling into America's deserts.

Emissaries of the U.S. Army then traveled to the Middle East to purchase camels and bring them back to America. No less than 75 camels were shipped over to Texas in this endeavor.

Almost immediately following their arrival, the camels were put to work. Two dozen camels were dispatched for an expedition into California run by Edward Fitzgerald Beale. Beale and his men put the camels to good use, running the camels over 1,000 miles through barren and hot deserts and up and down arid mountains.

Meanwhile, the remaining animals were put to work in Texas and along the Mexican border.

The camels were indeed proving to be useful animals in hot environments just as the War Department had predicted. But there was one industry sector that wasn't excited about the presence of camels in America in the slightest: the mule industry.

Representatives of the mule industry lobbied Congress hard to not bring any more camels into America. As a result, three proposals for Congress to buy more camels were shot down in the capital.

The final nail in the coffin for the camels was the outbreak of the Civil War. When Camp Verde in Texas, which was where most of the camels were being held, was seized by Confederate soldiers, the camels were allowed to roam free and graze.

One camel, however, was put to work. Named Old Douglas, he served with the 43rd Mississippi infantry regiment. Tragically, however, Old Douglas was shot and killed by a Union sniper from afar during the Siege of Vicksburg.

Several of the Confederate troopers serving in the regiment had grown emotionally attached to Old Douglas and decided to avenge him. After a burial for the poor animal, they managed to hunt down the sniper and kill him.

Meanwhile, the two dozen camels who had served in Beale's California expedition were being held by the Union military in Los Angeles. They had gone without work for more than a year, so Secretary of War Edwin Stanton ordered the animals to be auctioned off so the money could be used to help fund the war effort in early 1864.

A man named Samuel McLaughlin purchased the entire herd and put them to work in the salt mines of Nevada. He also set up camel races in Sacramento, which attracted an audience of thousands of people.

After their work in the salt mines, the remaining camels were then sold to zoos and circuses in California, but a few were even sold back to Beale, who put the animals to work on his ranch and would even ride the animals for fun.

Some camels ended up in Texas, others ended up in Mexico, and others stayed in California. Since they were allowed to breed, their population had slowly expanded beyond the 75 animals that had originally shipped in from the Middle East. Tracking the offspring of the camels, however, proved to be difficult.

Beale's personal camel, a unique white-haired specimen named Said, was killed in a battle for dominance by another camel in Beale's herd. Said's body was then shipped back to Washington D.C. where it would be preserved by the Smithsonian Institution.

It's an absolute certainty that at least a few camels wandered their way into the desert where they became feral. Sightings were sporadic throughout the late 1800s, with the Red Ghost being the most famous camel sighting by far and attracting national attention in the newspapers.

The only real question that remains is how long the feral camels managed to survive in the southwestern deserts before they gradually died off. At the very least, sightings continued well up into the late 1920s.

Ultimately, it was the mule industry and the U.S. Civil War that ended the camel experiment of the American military.

Had either of those events not happened, the use of camels would likely have become more widespread, as Congress was prepared to place more orders for more animals. And if that happened, camels would have become a wild species in western North America just as deer, elk, antelope, and wild boar are.

This is exactly what happened in Australia, for instance. Camels were introduced into Australia in 1840 (around the same time that they were brought into the United States) for the same purpose of being used as pack animals. Today, there are over a million camels living wild in the Australian Outback as a result.

That being said, the camels were not prized by everybody as pack animals. While it is true that the camels performed well in packing equipment and supplies over long distances in arid environments (as had been expected), the animals were also disliked by many Army soldiers for their foul stench and tendency to spit cud when they were angry or upset.

Nonetheless, the use of camels in the Old West is one of the most overlooked and unknown stories from that era. The legend of the Red Ghost also went down as one of the most bizarre myths that the Old West ever had to offer, and the

146

identity of the dead rider who was strapped to that particular camel's back persists as a mystery to this day.

The next set of stories that we'll dive into in our last chapter, however, is even more bizarre.

UFO SIGHTINGS IN THE OLD WEST

Throughout the 1800s — and many decades before Roswell - Native Americans and cowboys alike often reported sightings of craft in the air that closely mirror the UFO sightings from throughout the 1900s and into the 2000s. But do these sightings and the associated legends that came with them have any real merit?

It was initially just another day in Aurora, Texas, on April 17, 1897.

But what happened next sounds like it should have happened in Roswell 50 years later.

It was early in the morning when many people going about their daily lives in Aurora looked up into the sky and noticed what appeared to be a large flying craft cylindrically shaped like a cigar tube.

Keep in mind, Orville and Wilbur Wright wouldn't invent the first airplane until six years later. Hot air balloons had been around for over a hundred years, and some people had read Jules Verne science-fiction novels that involved hypothetical narratives about space travel in fanciful metal capsules, but the concept of aerial travel was still largely foreign to most folks at that time.

In this case, they were witnessing what appeared to be a metallic craft traveling at very high speeds through the air. It was unlike anything they could have even comprehended.

No one knows exactly what happened next because what occurred is so clouded in mystery and intrigue.

But according to witnesses, the metallic craft fell from the air and crashed directly into a windmill before exploding in a massive ball of fire! The windmill was on the property of Judge J.S. Proctor.

Even more mysterious is what happened directly afterwards.

Soldiers and military officials from a nearby military base descended over the area. The body of the pilot who had been in the craft was pulled out of the debris and buried, and the wreckage from the craft itself was disposed of in a nearby well.

And even more mysteriously, rumors soon spread that the pilot of the craft was an unidentified species that was either a "Martian" or something "not of this world." This was according to a report from a single officer at the local Army outpost. News of this supposed alien creature who was hastily buried afterward got out and the residents began to call the creature "Ned."

The entire incident - the supposed crashed spaceship, the alien pilot, and the quick military-involved coverup of the wreckage - sounds exactly like Roswell or any other modern-day UFO incident.

To this day, no one knows exactly what happened that day in Wise County, Texas. Some locals will insist to you that an alien spacecraft crashed into that windmill and was quickly covered up by the military. Others will claim that the entire story about Ned and the spacecraft is hogwash and was fabricated to bring tourists to help revive the economy.

But if you go to Aurora Cemetery today, you'll find a small historical marker acknowledging the event. And in the decades since, people have carefully searched the area looking for pieces of metal from the crash site that weren't scooped up and disposed of. In the 1970s, there was even an attempt to exhume the grave where Ned was supposed to be buried, but the cemetery's association filed a court injunction to stop it and subsequent efforts have also failed.

All of this only further added to the enigma and lent credence to the question: What happened at Aurora, Texas, on April 17, 1897?

When we think of UFO sightings, we normally think of them occurring in a more modern-day context. The concept of aliens and UFOs didn't start to capture the public's imagination until the 1950s after the Roswell crash and when science fiction movies started to get released and become popular.

But if you think about it, if reported sightings of UFOs and aliens were happening throughout the 20th century and up to today, perhaps similar sightings could have happened earlier.

The Aurora crash was not the only sighting supposedly involving spacecraft or aliens that occurred in the Old West. It was only one of many.

****

The idea of aliens visiting Earth and interacting with humans all over the world in our historical (and sometimes ancient) past has long intrigued humanity and has been the subject of countless books, movies, and TV shows.

For example, stories and legends of the "gods" descending from the "heavens" or the "stars" and teaching humans their secret knowledge have featured prominently in ancient Sumerian, Egyptian, and Indian legends and mythos. Some people today interpret these legends as merely stories, while others view them as reflecting fact and as how people living in ancient times explained alien visitations.

That being said, the Old American West is a specific period in history that has traditionally not received a great detail of attention when it comes to the concept of alien visitation and UFOs.

This is despite many Native American myths and legends involving "star people" and visitations from other worlds or dimensions -which many people have also interpreted as a way to explain alien visitation. There are not just a few myths and legends here and there. There are so many that it's nearly impossible to count them all!

For example, the Cree people from Canada have a legend that they come from the Pleiades star system, a group of more than 800 stars located over 400 lightyears away from Earth but still very visible in the night sky.

These legends have been passed down through the Cree people for many generations over the centuries. According to the Cree, the first "Star Woman" viewed Earth from another dimension. A hole in the sky was created, and she fell through it to land and become the first official human from the Earth.

Today, many Cree who are familiar with these legends will tell you that their people came from the stars.

It's not just the Cree. The Lakota, Hopi, and Zuni tribes, among many others, all have similar legends involving the "star people." The big debate today is whether these legends are meant to be taken literally, or if they would be deemed as folklore and a way for people to try and make sense of their origins and surroundings.

The Pleiades in particular is a star system that shows up in many Native American origin stories across many tribes.

According to the Lakota, for instance, there were once seven maidens who were chased by a bear. Feeling hopeless, the maidens dropped to their knees and prayed for intervention from the gods above.

Suddenly, the ground below the maidens erupted and carried them upward, and the bear attempted in vain to climb up the rock to reach them, forming distinct vertical marks over what is now known as Devil's Tower. The seven maidens, as the legend continued, then ascended upward to become the Pleiades.

According to a Hopi legend, their ancestors were not of this world. The Hopi believe there was a people who lived in the worlds of the Pleiades, which they called the Chuhukon (translated as "those who cling together"). Eventually, these people came to Earth, but to this day, the Hopi can call on "Kachinas" who still travel between the Chuhukon and the Earth and provide them guidance.

The Kachinas, the Hopi believe, taught their ancestors their religion and how to hunt and live off of the land. The Hopi Home Dance, which is held at the end of the Hopi religious calendar, commemorates the return of the Kachinas to Chuhukon.

The Kachinas of the Hopi are interpreted by some today as being either aliens or beings from another realm or dimension.

Were these legends real?

****

Wallace Black Elk was a Lakota spiritual elder who lived from 1921 to 2004. He was a descendant of Nicholas Black Elk, another Lakota Elder who was known for recounting the detailed spiritual visions he often experienced.

Wallace Black Elk wrote a book called *Black Elk: The Sacred Ways of the Lakota* in which he claimed to have communicated with extraterrestrials and even witnessed a UFO falling out of the sky.

"So, when I went to vision quest, that disk came from above," said Black Elk. "The scientists call that an…Unidentified Flying Object, but that's a joke, see? Because they are not trained, they lose contact with wisdom, power and gift…. So that disk landed on top of me. It was concave, and there was another one on top of that. It was silent, but it lit and luminesced like neon lights. Even the sacred robes there were luminesced, and those tobacco ties lying there lit up like little light bulbs. Then these little people came, but each little group spoke a different language. They could read minds, and I could read their minds. I could read them. So, there was silent communication. You could read it, like when you read silent symbols in a book. So, we were able to communicate…They are human, so I welcomed them. I said, 'Welcome.'"

Black Elk also claimed that his visions revealed that human beings adopted the religious teachings of aliens in the distant past. Furthermore, Black Elk claimed that the aliens actually worked to "upgrade" humans on a spiritual and physical level, and he even went as far as to say that all humans are "part alien."

Many Native American legends speak of similar interactions with beings from other dimensions. There are numerous Native American myths of "star people" traveling from other worlds or "light beings" who come from other dimensions. Sometimes, these beings are benevolent and teach humans how to live off of the land and about the intricacies of the spiritual realm.

But other times, the beings are malevolent and abduct children. If true, these stories would correlate very closely with the stories of alien abductions that are commonly discussed today.

The Zuni people also have direct references to people from other worlds in their own mythologies and origin stories. According to Zuni tradition, their ancestors from thousands of years ago (at the beginning of the "fourth world," in the Zuni timeline) had direct contact with "beings from space." In some versions of the legends, these beings from space had come down to earth in round-shaped objects or great balls of light. According to the Zuni, these beings were their original teachers.

These Native American legends involving visitations from the star people are not just reflected in their writings or their oral traditions, but also their art. There are numerous petroglyphs across the Southwest, for instance, that depict humanoid entities that look "alien" or unlike anything else that we have seen elsewhere.

Petroglyphs like these are a common fixture in the rock formations in Utah, having been carved into stone by members of the Navajo tribe, specifically in the Uinta Basin. This area is also a hotbed for bizarre reports of cattle mutilations, alien visitations, UFO sightings, and other strange and paranormal occurrences. These occurrences have featured prominently in Navajo folklore and legend for hundreds of years as well.

****

The concept of UFOs and extraterrestrials in the Old West may seem rather odd, but that's only because other events from that time and place, such as the ones we've talked about earlier, have drawn much of the focus.

But it's clear that the concept of earthly visitations by people from other worlds formed a major part of the origin stories and oral histories for many Western Native American tribes and helped to shape their religious beliefs and practices.

Was there really an alien spaceship that crashed in Aurora in 1897? Do the Native American myths and legends really talk about literal visitations from beings of other worlds? And if so to both, is there a relation between the two, and then can we take that relation and connect it to modern-day legends of UFO and alien sightings today?

In due time, perhaps, more research and more findings will hopefully lead to more answers. Until then, all we can do is speculate.

CONCLUSION

The Old American West wasn't exactly the glorious or romantic place that many people might imagine it to be. It was a gritty, brutal, and unforgiving place where people sought to create their destinies by finding fame, adventure, riches, or just a new way of life. Some like John Chisum found the opportunity they were looking for, while many others like George Custer met their violent demise.

The stories of the Old West that we've shared in this book have endured because they come from a land and era that was largely lawless, meaning the people who lived back then had to live vastly different lives than we do today.

We can't help but think about what we would do if we lived in those times. Imagine yourself as a lawman, an outlaw, a rancher, a farmer, a prospector, or even just a business shop owner living in a lawless town and think about what life would be like. It was a drastically different world back then.

Back then, people often had to forge their own way, take the law into their own hands, and brave unforgiving horrors in their daily efforts just to stay alive. The Old West was a place where people went to plan and shape their own destinies but often became victims to violent fate instead.

Look no further than Wyatt Earp or Geronimo. These men wanted nothing more than to create a peaceful destiny for themselves, Wyatt Earp as a businessman trying to escape his past as a law enforcement officer and Geronimo as a medicine man in the deserts of Arizona with his wife and children.

Instead, fate wrested the planned destinies from both men. They were forced to sidestep the law and take matters into their own hands to avenge their loved ones. Both of these men displayed remarkable courage and bravery against overwhelming odds in the process. Wyatt Earp and his small posse regularly took on enemy forces that were many times their size, while Geronimo had no combat experience when he assembled his war party to avenge his family's brutal murder.

Both Wyatt Earp and Geronimo may have lived very different lives, but they were unable to escape the violence that fate had in store for them despite their desires for peace.

There were also many men, like Billy the Kid or Jesse James, who took advantage of this lawlessness for their own purposes to create their destinies. Modern-day law enforcement surveillance and equipment did not exist back then, which is why outlaws and robbers got away with a lot more than they could today. An outlaw would only need to have a good gun to force the bank teller to open the safe and a good horse to quickly ride out of town to commit their crimes.

Billy the Kid and Jesse James were both very successful in their criminal careers…, at least while they were alive. Not even these men, who both had a serious knack for being able to outdraw or evade law enforcement and other men sent to kill them, could escape their own violent fates in the end. As the old saying goes, those who live by the gun often die by the gun, and this proved to be true for men like Billy the Kid and Jesse James.

And then there were the passionate and unpredictable people, like Wild Bill Hickok or Calamity Jane, who helped make the Old West become known as the "Wild West." Wild Bill and Calamity Jane both had strong personalities that helped give them the confidence they needed to achieve their many accomplishments in their respective lives.

But fate wouldn't allow either of them to escape, with Wild Bill falling at a young age to the gun and Calamity Jane slowly dying due to the bottle.

But perhaps the biggest reason why these stories from the Old West have endured through the ages is because of the mystery that surrounds them.

No one knows for sure, for example, who killed Johnny Ringo in the Earp Vendetta Ride, whether Billy the Kid really got away or not, whether Jesse James' assassination was planned by the Governor of Missouri, who the dead rider was atop the Red Ghost camel, or what exactly crashed in Aurora, Texas.

These mysteries may very well remain so for the rest of eternity, and if they do, that means that the Old West will likely become even more renowned as time goes on and new theories to explain these mysteries emerge.

The inherently unruly and sometimes ungovernable nature of the Old West combined with the legend and mystery that surrounds it is what makes it one of the most memorable and compelling eras in American history.

As Wyatt Earp once said, "Destiny is that which we are drawn toward, and fate is that which we run into."

Sure enough, people in those days headed to the "Wild West" because they were drawn to an idea of destiny they had in their hearts and minds - but they ran into fate instead.

Printed in Great Britain
by Amazon

47849407R00096